About the Author

Pauline Wilson lives in Yarrawonga in North East Victoria on the banks of the Murray River. A writer and passionate family historian, she brings the stories of her ancestors to life through historical fiction rich in research and emotion. Her novels explore the courage, challenges and everyday heroism of ordinary people making extraordinary choices. When she's not diving into archives, Pauline enjoys reading and long walks by the river.

Pauline has written three historical fiction books. This is her first non-fiction book based on her quest to become a self-published author.

Connect on Instagram (@paulinemareewilson) or Facebook (@paulinewilsonauthor)

Also by

Conflict at Hanging Rock

Breaking Free

Family & Fortune

To stay updated on my latest releases and all my news, sign up

to my newsletter.

www.paulinewilson.com.au/news

Becoming an Indie Author

Finding voice and courage on the road
to independent authorship

Pauline Wilson

Boughyards Press

First published by Boughyards Press in 2026

A catalogue record for this book is available from the National Library of Australia

Cover design by Douglas Thomson at High Voltage Studio

Contents

Part 1: Beginnings

Boughyards Press

Introduction

The cursor blinks relentlessly, daring me to begin. The blank page. The bane of every writer.

You would think that after publishing three books, starting a new manuscript would not be so daunting. But here I am again, staring at the blinking cursor, feeling that familiar mix of trepidation and excitement. My first novel sits proudly in my bookcase along with the two I have written since. They are proof that I can write and publish a full-length book. Yet I still don't feel confident that my fourth book will ever eventuate. It seemed impossible the first time and doesn't feel any easier now.

So many times along this journey I have almost given up. Fear tried to hold me back in so many ways. I had put in the hard yards and thought I had the basic knowledge required to write and publish a book. I was learning the writing craft and the technology needed to publish my books, but each time I had to click that final button to finish a process, I hesitated, trepidation gripping me. However, I persistently refused to allow fear to dominate.

Each new project brings its own unique challenges, its own moments of self-doubt. The dread of facing the blank page never goes away. But I now know that the blinking cursor is my friend; it's just waiting for me to begin the journey once again.

I am clearly not doing this for the money. Apparently, the average annual earnings for authors in Australia is only around $15,000. This figure is still way out of reach for me. In fact, my writing is still an expensive hobby at this stage. Add to that the fact that the market is saturated with millions of great quality books, so there are no guarantees that I will sell any of my books. But something keeps drawing me back to that blinking cursor. The same thing that drove me to write the first three books; that is, the simple desire to record the stories of my ancestors in a way that appeals to a wide audience.

Now to my current work, this book. I began writing with the sole aim of telling family stories, but as I struggled to learn all the things I needed to know in order to become a published author, I started journalling about the process, which made me wonder whether others might be interested in knowing about my journey. Would this account of how I came to be a published author, at the age of 64, help others on their own journeys?

What began as simple notetaking; jotting down the challenges, the victories, the moments of despair and of success, evolved into something more meaningful. I found myself documenting not just the practical steps of becoming an author, but the emotions experienced along the way: the vulnerability of sharing my work for the first time, the thrill of holding my first printed book, the challenges of marketing and self-promotion.

I don't intend this to be a step-by-step guide. There are plenty of excellent resources available for that purpose. Rather, it is a personal account of what it feels like to take a new direction as an author and how I came to do that later in life. It's about discovering that age isn't a barrier to pursuing your dreams. My focus is not on instruction but rather on experience.

I want to share the reality of what it means to become an author; not just the success stories, but the messy parts as well. The moments of self-doubt, the massive learning curve that sometimes felt more like a steep rise than a curve and the persistence required to keep going when confidence wavered. Because maybe, just maybe, my story might resonate with someone else who is at the beginning of their own writing journey, wondering whether they too can transform their dreams into reality.

In this book, I will take you along with me through each phase as I transformed from aspiring writer to published author. I will break down the process for each book to show that sometimes I learned from my mistakes and sometimes I made the same mistakes again.

I will show how I navigated each stage through the maze of decisions that I had to make. I will share the milestones along the way, including the day I typed 'The End' on my first draft, only to realise it was really just the beginning. Being an author is an emotional roller coaster. The ups and downs of writing, editing, creating a website, building my author platform, and the technical aspects of formatting and publishing have certainly taken me on a ride.

I'll reveal the true costs, both financial and emotional, of bringing a book to life. From the tools that provided so much help, to the marketing strategies that pushed me way outside my comfort zone. Although my path to becoming an author may be unique to me, the fundamental challenges and triumphs are universal. Whilst I acknowledge that everyone's journey is different, I will share what worked for me in the key takeaways at the end of each chapter.

This isn't just about the mechanics of publishing a book – though you'll find plenty of that here. It's about the transformation that happens when you decide to chase a dream, regardless of your age or experience. It's about discovering that becoming an author involves so much more than just writing words on a page.

This book is for anyone who has quietly wondered whether it might be too late to start a new career as an author. It is for people who love stories but are unsure whether they have the right background or skills. For those who have reached a point in their lives where starting something new feels equally exciting and terrifying.

Five years ago, I was working full time with a dream to retire and tell my family stories. Today, I'm a published author with three books to my name. The distance between those two points isn't measured in years or words – it's measured in determination, persistence, and quite a few glasses of bubbles.

Finding My Voice

Have you ever had a dream you wanted to pursue, but thought that time had passed you by? Many people dream of one day writing a novel. Some get on and do it, but most don't. I have heard a lot of female authors say that they wrote their first book when they were on maternity leave. So, that is, they started quite young. Not so for me. I first started thinking about writing a book in my early 50s. Although always a keen reader, before this I had no desire to become a writer, let alone a published author. When I came to the realisation that I wanted to write a book, I asked myself if I had waited too long.

Most people who contemplate becoming an author are avid readers. In this way I was no different. Like many others of my generation, I was a huge fan of Enid Blyton's books and read each book many times over. I particularly loved the mystery books: ***The Secret Seven, The Famous Five, The Five Find-Outers***.

In my teenage years, I mainly read books that were on the school English curriculum. Most were classics, which at the time I did not appreciate. Sometimes I think the way we had to analyse these books destroyed our enjoyment of them. Or perhaps it was just that I was too immature to comprehend them. I have read several classics as an adult and found that I enjoyed them much more. Books like ***A Tale of Two Cities***, ***Jane Eyre***, and ***Wuthering Heights***. Lately, I have broadened my reading list, focusing on a wide variety of genres and I have read more classics as part of the research for my third novel.

As a young adult, I read a lot of crime, mostly by Agatha Christie. I still have an enormous pile of her books that I have never felt able to dispose of. Other authors I read included Ngaio Marsh, Dorothy Sayers and, more recently, P. D. James. I still love a good crime or cosy mystery and have recently read many modern crime novels by exceptional Australian authors, including Michael Robotham, Chris Hammer, Pamela Hart, Amanda Hampson and the list goes on.

Fortunately, I still love reading. I could honestly sit and read all day. But I am not sure where the idea came from that I could write a full-length book.

Some would consider it a bit late to get serious about a writing career in my 60s. Being a writer had never been something I had thought about. Many authors have had dreams of being a writer all their lives. That was also not me. I do consider that I am creative though. Over the years I have had many creative pursuits. I love music and learnt to play the piano. In later years I also learned to play the guitar and a group of us played and sang at church. I also did a lot of sewing, creating all sorts of children's clothes and I made most of my own clothes. Then there was knitting, crochet and embroidery. I never learnt to draw which is something that is still on my to do list. Although writing was never something I thought about a lot, when I think back, I have been writing for many years and in many styles and genres.

Of course, at school there were essays and tests to write. My final year at school included a lot of historical writing and English essays. That is where my love of history began.

As a child, I always wanted to be a teacher, so I went on to Teacher's College, as it was called back in the day. More writing ensued, which I also enjoyed. However, the pathway got a bit twisted, and I didn't end up finishing Teacher's College. Instead, I got married and had kids. At that point, I pursued many other interests and became a swimming teacher and coach as well. Still lots of learning, reading and writing. I also wrote extensive travel diaries whenever we went on family holidays.

And then, a twist of fate meant that I had to take up the mantle of breadwinner in our family. At nearly 50 years of age, I applied for a job that I felt I had no qualifications for and, to my surprise, I was successful.

This was the start of my move into the world of Adult Education. All of a sudden, I had found what I wanted to do when I grew up. It is such a rewarding industry, seeing people achieve goals they had never imagined they were capable of. I started on a huge learning adventure, which eventually saw me achieve several Vocational Education and Training qualifications from Certificate II up to Diploma level. By now I was writing learning materials and all manner of business documents such as reports, grant applications and acquittals. So much writing.

At about the time I entered the world of Adult Education, the concept of Web 2.0 was exploding. There was so much exciting technology to explore, where the adventurous among us were actually starting to interact with the internet as opposed to just using it to find information. I was offered an opportunity to undertake an e-learning mentorship. I think it is safe to say that this changed my life. At the time, there was only very limited use of technology in the Adult Community Education sector in which I worked. But for some reason I took to it like a duck to water. The apps were mostly free, so we could experiment and play with them all. I started using some of the tools to create new learning materials and used wikis and blogs to house these artefacts. Blogs were just coming into their own at this time, and I started reporting on projects in blog posts.

After exploring this new world for a while, I decided it was time to write my own blog. As part of my work in the Adult Education sector, I was a member of a team who designed a course called Reflect and Connect, and I took part in the pilot to trial the course. My blog was called *Reflections and Connections*. I had already learned so much. Now it was time to reflect and consolidate some of my learning. *Reflections and Connections* started out as a place to record my reflective practice but soon morphed into much more. I wrote about anything new that I was learning, my holidays and travel, in fact anything that I felt the need to record. I have written many thousands of words in my blogs over the ensuing years.

I guess that made me a writer. Now I wanted to find out whether I could become a published author.

Having started to think about writing a full-length book, I could not see where I would find the time. I had many things taking priority. Not that I am pretending this is an excuse. In the busyness of life, it never occurred to me I could squeeze in writing time as well, but I found a way. Then, at the end of 2020, I retired from my full-time job and finished up a couple of other voluntary positions. Freeing up some time allowed me to concentrate more on my writing.

There are many reasons someone wants to become an author, but I think one of the most noted ones is that they have a story to tell. I definitely had a story to tell. In fact, there were so many fascinating stories that have been passed down to me and that I have spent many years researching.

Family history became a passion for me many years ago. Through this pastime, which quickly became somewhat of an obsession, I discovered a love of research, focusing on the social history of the places my family settled when they came to Australia. The stories my father told of his Irish ancestors were the initial inspiration for my research. He was a wonderful storyteller, weaving in their superstitions and peculiar habits. Fortunately, my interest developed whilst he was still alive, and I am so grateful I had the foresight to record his stories, both in audio and written format.

When I first began writing the stories, it was with the sole motive of recording all the research I had done over many years. Otherwise, what was to become of it? Family historians know that unless they share it, research often becomes piles of paper in folders or files on computers. Having done so much work over the years, I wanted my research to live beyond the filing cabinets, so I began turning my files into stories that my family would be more likely to read and hopefully enjoy.

This is where my inspiration to become a published author came from. For me, genealogy is not just about charts and dates. It is about the stories hidden behind those names and dates.

Little did I know that my obsession with recording family stories would lead to a fully-fledged author career.

Part 2: Inspiration and Research

Boughyards Press

Family Stories as Inspiration

I commenced work on a manuscript in 2017, armed with the research I had undertaken up until that point. The working title of this manuscript is 'Grandma's Rose'. I have added to it from time to time, but at present it contains about 13,000 words and sits idle, still waiting to be finished. When I get back to it, this project will chronicle the story of each of my four grandparents, their ancestors and descendants. As with all stories, I needed to set some parameters around the timelines for this manuscript, so the plan is to begin the story of each branch of the family when the first of my ancestors came to Australia. I have not done a lot of research into the times before my ancestors immigrated, so it made sense to make people who had come to Australia the boundary for this manuscript. Of course, I plan to provide some background on their origins, but the stories will primarily take place in Australia. This manuscript is intended to be a totally factual version of my family history, telling just the facts as I know them. Of course, I hope to get it finished one day if only to be read by family and to be a record of my years of research. However, knowing that this work would not be interesting to anyone except family members, I began to ponder how I could make the stories appeal to a wider audience.

In 2018, I learned about the Diploma of Family History being offered by the University of Tasmania. I enrolled in the course and embarked on what was to be a very special learning experience. It provided so many great resources and ideas about where and how to research.

I had always imagined that family history stories would have to be written as non-fiction, including only the known and referenced facts, but during the course I discovered the genre of creative non-fiction where dialogue, narrative arcs and vivid imagery is added to tell true stories. I wrote my first creative non-fiction piece about my great-grandmother's grief at the loss of her son. This sparked something in me. I really wanted to fill in the gaps in the stories. Despite all efforts to research our ancestors, we can only discover so much, and gaps will always exist. By writing creative non-fiction, I felt I could get into my ancestors' heads and imagine what everyday life would have been like for them.

I received positive feedback for some of the stories I submitted. This made me think that perhaps I did have enough skill to get serious about writing full-length novels. Little did I know how much I still had to learn. But in the meantime, I wanted to publish the stories in some form, so I started another blog called

A Genealogy Journey, where I posted the stories I was writing for the course.

Once I finished the diploma, I concluded I would like to write stories that appealed to a wider audience, not just for my family. I set myself the goal of helping people understand that family history does not have to be boring. I am well aware of how many people's eyes glaze over when the topic arises. But I am of the firm belief that this is because much family history is just a collection of facts such as births, deaths and marriages. I wanted to correct that impression by bringing my ancestors' stories to life. I knew that to appeal to readers who don't have a connection to my family, I would need to include events and incidents that are not completely factual. But I believed that incorporating what I found in my research on the social history of the time and place, would make my stories reflect what could realistically have happened. When I studied history at school, Australian history was always lacking in the curriculum. Perhaps my work could be a way for people to learn more about 19th-century Australia. I had to work out how I could achieve this rather lofty goal.

I read a fantastic book by Nick Brodie called **Kin**. It placed his family squarely in the times when they lived, adding the social history of the era. What a wonderful book! He doesn't attempt to tell the story of his entire family tree. But rather, he picks out some branches of his family who lived in particularly interesting times or places. For example, those who were around when Ned Kelly roamed the bush in North East

Victoria. Perhaps I could write a similar book, fitting in some of my own family branches. Would that be appropriate? Or would I be plagiarising someone else's idea? However, I know that many books have similar elements. It is the unique and individual ideas and stories that sit with the author that should come through.

I guess that is something that all would-be authors need to consider. Will my story be unique, or am I telling the same story that others have already told? Many stories are of the same genre and follow similar tropes. I wasn't sure how I could ensure mine would be unique. But I know everyone has a story to tell, and everyone will put their own stamp on a particular piece of work. No two people will ever write exactly the same story. As my writing has evolved, I have found I do have my own voice, and I intend to continue working to develop it.

I originally thought my first project would be in a similar vein to *Kin*. But that was when I discovered more about some of my convict ancestors. There was no shortage of factual information about them, their crimes and their many family disputes. It was a story that needed to be told. Consequently, I had found the subject for my first book.

Which brings me to the major decision I had to struggle with. I wasn't sure whether to just try to write this story as a fully factual account. After considerable thought, I decided that would not do the story justice because there were too many gaps in the facts as I knew them at that time. Of course, more research would no doubt unearth more facts. After all, family stories are never completely researched.

I then faced another dilemma. Whilst doing the research about one particular branch of my family for what was to become **Conflict at Hanging Rock**, I found a history written by one of their descendants, which seemed to indicate that these ancestors were fine upstanding citizens of the Hanging Rock community. That gave me pause and made me question whether it might be better to write the story as fiction, fearing that I might upset some living descendants.

I wondered if perhaps I should write the book as creative non-fiction and embellish the bits that were known. I still had a lot to learn about writing creative non-fiction, so I did not feel confident in doing that.

My ultimate decision was to write this first story as fiction, based on or inspired by the true stories, changing all the names, with the exception of one or two peripheral characters, whose names are real. I made the same decision with my subsequent books.

But even in deciding to write the stories as fiction, I was torn between the need to tell the true story as far as possible and the need to make it an engaging read. Sisters and authors, Kate Forsyth and Belinda Murrell, talk about this very difficulty in the telling of their 4x great-grandmother's story in the book they co-authored, **Searching for Charlotte**. Kate and Belinda grappled with the problem of not wanting to get it wrong. When discussing this in the book, they describe a meeting with

Emma Darwin, a descendant of Charles Darwin. Emma wrote a book called **'This is Not a Book about Charles Darwin'**. In it, she says her book is *"strung painfully on the tension-line between the responsibilities of the storyteller and the responsibilities of the historian."* That statement really resonated with me.

Despite my eventual decision to write fiction, I tried to stick to the facts as closely as possible. This determination was sometimes to the detriment of my story, as I am sure my editors would tell you. I must say they were extremely patient with me as they tried to help me find ways to tell an entertaining story whilst still sticking to the facts.

I started my first book in late 2019 shortly after submitting my final assessment for the Diploma of Family History and published *Conflict at Hanging Rock* in June 2022. It took me two and a half years to get it to a standard that I felt comfortable with. Since then I have published two more novels, **Breaking Free** in November 2023 and **Family & Fortune** in March 2025.

Key Takeaways:

- Everyone is or can be a writer if they want to be.

- Family history is not dull or ordinary. Dig deeper to find the interesting family stories.

- There are numerous ways to tell family stories. *Kin* and *Searching for Charlotte* are two perfect examples.

The Joy (and Trap) of Research

Writing historical fiction requires extensive research. With my books being set in the 19th century I have limited knowledge of the world my ancestors lived in. I need to delve deeply into the period to make my stories realistic and bring my characters to life. Research is a very time-consuming part of the novel writing process, but it is a large part of what I enjoy about writing these stories. I love digging into the archives. I sometimes feel that I enjoy the research more than the writing.

I like to complete most of the research before the writing begins. It helps that I have been delving into my family history for many years, so some facts are close at hand. Other aspects need much more work. I have found that rather than just doing the research, I prefer to actually study and learn the relevant history, much as you would for an exam. I think the story flows more easily if I have the facts embedded in my mind rather than having to keep looking things up as I write. But as the story unfolds there are always new ideas that crop up and need additional research. Once I start writing, I like to try to keep going through to the end of the first draft before going down too many rabbit holes. It is way too easy to get sidetracked, so I like to make a note and come back to it later. But on occasions I really feel that I can't go on until I do that little bit of extra research that I need to continue with the story.

When writing historical fiction, the settings and characters need to be accurate for the time and place. For me, it is incredibly important to get this part right. Imagine if you were reading a book about the 1950s and someone had a mobile phone. I don't know about you, but I would immediately be pulled out of the story. That is an extreme example, but people who are interested in history and have read other historical fiction books will soon spot it if the research is not thorough.

Being a family historian for about 15 years, I have learnt a lot about research, and completing the Diploma of Family History taught me a lot more. Although I now know quite a bit about research, there is always more to learn. My wonderful family history group, who are also alumni of the Diploma of Family History, has shown me a lot of other resources. So, for me, the research is almost second nature.

So far, I have mostly set my stories in 19th century Australia, in Victoria. This helps with the research because I have learnt quite a lot about this period, and as each story begins, I have some knowledge about the time and place.

Since I write family stories, I discovered many of my resources on Ancestry.com, a paid subscription service. I think having access to genealogy sites is worth paying for, particularly for family historians, but also for historical writers. Other genealogy sites are My Heritage, Find My Past and the free site administered by the Church of Latter Day Saints, Family Search. Sites such as these provide access to a lot of important background and records. I have used many of them, but Ancestry is the one I use most.

When I research social history to insert into my story, I always begin with a simple Google search. That often leads to Wikipedia, which is an amazing source of basic information, but like all secondary sources, it needs to be verified to ensure accuracy. It contains links to other useful sources, so I find it a good starting point before moving onto other resources.

When I am getting started on a new project, I usually also create a Pinterest board where I post images to create a visual representation of parts of the story.

One of the best pieces of advice about research is to use primary sources where possible. This is where Trove becomes so important. Trove contains digital copies of a wealth of Australian newspapers, magazines and many other artefacts. Currently, there are over 14 billion digital items easily accessed for free! We are so lucky to have such a fantastic resource in Australia. In other countries, newspaper archives and the like often come with a fee.

Other sources of primary documents that I have used include those found in the National and State Libraries and the Public Record Office of Victoria. Libraries Tasmania has fantastic resources on convicts. Historical societies and family history societies are another significant source of well-researched information.

But I never rely on the first source of information I find. I always seek out several sources for each detail I plan to use in my stories, comparing accounts to ensure accuracy I look for primary materials – such as letters, diaries, and photographs – whenever possible, as they offer a direct glimpse into the past. For example, with ancestors common names it can be difficult to ensure that I have the correct person. By finding a date of birth on two separate primary documents I can be more certain I have found the correct family member. Other sources can include history books, academic journals, old newspapers, museum archives, and reputable online databases. By drawing from a wide range of resources, I can build a richer, more authentic picture of the world I'm writing about.

The final piece in the research puzzle for me is to visit the places where my stories are set. Fortunately, most places where my family settled are close to home, so I have been able to visit.

Each of my books needed a great deal of research, which was slightly different for each one. Sometimes there was plenty of factual information to be found, other times, not so much.

Conflict at Hanging Rock (published July 2022)

This book tells the story of my great, great, great grandfather who was sentenced to seven years' transportation but who, in a twist of fate, arrived in Port Phillip with his ticket of leave after having only served two years of his sentence. His family soon followed him, and they settled at Hanging Rock in central Victoria. They were convicts and councillors, there were conflicts both in the family and within the community they called home.

As I researched this branch of my family, I found that there was a lot of information about them in the newspapers of the time. It seemed this particular branch of my family was quite volatile. There were a number of stories about their family disputes and court cases in the local papers. But in addition to these, I found reports in the British Newspaper Archives, which chronicled the crimes they had committed, resulting in two of them being transported to Australia. There was one particularly provocative article in the Shrewsbury Chronicle, dated April 4, 1845. It stated that they were "*A family long known as living chiefly by plunder and were always a terror to the neighbourhood*". It goes on to say that there were five members of the family currently in goal – all of them related to my great, great, great, grandfather.

The other branch of my family that features in this book is quite a contrast, being Particular Baptists who were highly religious. They brought their religion with them from the city and were instrumental in building the Baptist church that still stands today.

The two families were on opposite sides of the conflict about how the community should use the land at Hanging Rock.

Apart from the newspapers, I spent many hours finding and reading other sources of social history of the area. I purchased several history books written by members of the Woodend and District Heritage Society, which were very helpful. I also had a family history book written by Graeme Cook from which I was able to glean useful information about the religious branch of the family. But Chris McConville's excellent book, **Hanging Rock - A History**, was the most valuable source.

There are so many resources available online now that one could write a historical fiction novel without ever having to leave the house. However, I think it makes a huge difference to at least visit some of the places that are or could be the setting for my novels.

It has always been a wondrous feeling to visit Hanging Rock. The place has a mystical feel about it and is an important site for the Wurundjeri, Dja Dja Wurrung and Taungurung peoples, who have been the caretakers of the land around Hanging Rock for millennia. The rock was formed millions of years ago by lava oozing out of the ground, where it solidified. As a child, I attended the New Year's Day Picnic Races with my family. We have renewed this tradition in recent times, attending the horse races still held there on New Year's Day. But to climb to the summit of the rock, passing under the actual hanging rock, a boulder suspended between two larger boulders, gives a feeling of wonder and awe.

I have visited this location of my first book frequently. Looking up at the rock, wandering through the surrounding townships and seeing the old church that was built by my ancestors, enriched my book enormously.

Even though I published the book several years ago, it doesn't mean I stop learning about the area where my ancestors settled each time I visit. I recently found the location of their farm from the local shire heritage records and paid a visit to that site to stand where my ancestors stood. It was such a surreal feeling.

Breaking Free (Published November 2023)

As I began to research my second book, I was quite pleased that it was set in the same century and the same rural Victorian and Melbourne setting as the first book. So, I had some idea of the way things were. That cut down research time a bit.

The first source for this novel was a record of my great-grandmother's incarceration in the Kew Lunatic Asylum on March 15, 1894. The record was sparse, saying only that she had been *brought in by police* and was diagnosed with *mania caused by religious excitement.* It was also noted that she herself said that she had been *sent there by a good spirit.* There were only two more entries on her record, apart from the discharge note, for the entire 8 months of her incarceration. The first one read:

Report dated March 19, 1894

Bodily health not improving, restless, noisy, excited and violent, has to be fed. Transferred to the refractory ward, threatening violence to other patients.

Several weeks later, there was this note:

Report dated May 25, 1894

Bodily health improving, has become dull and stupid, in a mild stuporous state.

And finally, there was a note that she was *discharged on October 24, 1894.*

Once again I found plenty of information about life in an asylum at the time through the newspapers in Trove. 'The Vagabond', an anonymous reporter, gained employment in the asylum for a period of time and wrote extensively for the newspapers of his experiences.

I also found an article written by a woman who worked in the asylum, whose byline was simply 'An Attendant.'

I visited the Kew Lunatic Asylum, which is now the Willsmere Residential Estate. Even though I couldn't go inside, I got a feeling of the enormity and grandeur of the building. Imagine finding yourself at the gates of that imposing building with barred windows and lofty towers as a mental inmate.

I also spent a couple of days in the town of Avoca, where my ancestors lived at that time, visiting the Timor Grand Duke Mine where my great-great-grandfather worked. Once again, the locations all had an effect on me and the way I was able to visualise the setting for my book. Just one example was the school in Avoca. I was able to establish that it would have been the very same school that Annie would have attended. You can see a photograph of it on my website. Seeing the school allowed me to describe the distinctive looking building in the book.

'The school was a big imposing building with a turret-like roof. To Annie it looked like a castle from one of the fairy storybooks she liked to read.'

Family & Fortune (Published March 2025)

My third book begins in Bedfordshire, England, which created a whole new challenge. Unfortunately, as much as I would have liked to, I was unable to arrange a research trip. I knew little about Bedfordshire at that time, so the research was intense. One thing that I found incredibly useful was reading books written in the same time period as my books are set. I read **Hard Times**, **The Mayor of Casterbridge** and **Far from the Madding Crowd**. These books were instrumental in helping to set the scene. For example, I came across the term thimblerigger. I don't think any amount of research would necessarily have turned up that term, so I would not have been able to add the interesting dimension to the young Mary Ann's visit to the village fair. Young children of the time would have watched on in amazement as this confidence trickster moved his cups and the people who paid their money had to guess which cup the pea was under.

I also put in a research request to the Castlemaine Historical Society, and they provided me with a wealth of information, including a wonderful account of an interview with my great-great-grand aunt, Lily. Lily was 100 years of age when this interview took place, and she recalled many aspects of her childhood, which became incredibly important in my story. Many generous volunteers, who are members of historical societies, will take on research projects such as this for a reasonable fee.

Although I wasn't able to go to England, I did spend some time in Castlemaine with my husband and daughter. Whilst there, I was wandering around the Castlemaine Vintage Bazaar when I came across a book – a brief history called ***Castlemaine - A Golden Harvest*** written by Raymond Bradfield. Not expecting to find anything other than some social history, I took a chance and looked for the family name in the index. Sure enough, there it was.

The short passage about my family reads as follows:

(Richard) was one of the first men on Moonlight, and he did very well. He decided to go 'home' and bring out his bride. (Mary Ann) was only twenty-two years old when she arrived in Moonlight, and together they built their home of stone rubble, taken from the immediate locality. (Richard) found that the alluvial had been well worked over while he was away on his trip home, and although he could still make a living, it was a hard life, and not easy to make ends meet. He died at a fairly early age, but (Mary Ann) lived on to a grand old age, over a hundred years.

You can imagine my delight at finding this small passage, given that it supported everything I had found in my research.

During my research, I found a map of a mining license in Richard's name and also discovered that there was a road with the family name in the same area of Moonlight Flats. Of course, I had to see if I could find it. My family and I drove a short distance out of Castlemaine, and I was excited to see an old signpost still in place marking the road. We turned up the road, which was in fact just a rough unmade track, and after driving a short distance we came upon the ruins of a stone building. I have no proof that this was the stone cottage my great-great-great-grandparents built, but I like to believe that it is.

My main male character was a convict who was sentenced to seven years' transportation to Van Diemen's Land. The convict records are incredibly extensive, right down to eye colour and distinguishing marks. So, I was able to find out quite a lot about him and where he was stationed during his time as a convict.

By now it might be obvious that all my novels so far have grown out of some unusual happening in connection with my ancestors. A convict who arrives in Port Phillip with a ticket of leave, a 19-year-old woman incarcerated in a mental asylum and a mysterious return 'home' for marriage. I have found so much material to write what I hope are interesting stories by exploring my family history. I still have plenty of fodder for new stories, so for the moment my main genre will continue to be historical fiction.

I often find myself getting into the weeds with my research, finding information that is interesting, but adds nothing to the story. There is always so much more to learn than finds its way into a book. I have to be careful not to include interesting background that does not add to the story. For example, when I was researching *Breaking Free* I read copious newspaper articles from both the Vagabond and the anonymous female journalist who both worked in the Kew Asylum. But, even though it was interesting and informative and gave me a good background about what it would have been like to be incarcerated in an asylum at that time, it didn't progress Annie's story to include any more detail.

Additionally, it can be hard to know when enough is enough. Because I enjoy it so much, I need to remember that at some point, the research needs to end and the real work of writing the book needs to start. But what about researching a non-fiction book?

Becoming an Indie Author

This book has developed somewhat of an identity crisis. I think it's somewhere between a memoir and a reference book. As previously stated, I wasn't intending it to be a how-to book. But as I wrote I discovered that I did have something to offer as far as advice to other authors. I have made plenty of mistakes and perhaps my experiences will help others not to make the same mistakes. Given that this book is partly memoir, relating to my own experiences, the research required was a lot less than for my historical fiction. Perhaps if I hadn't been keeping a journal, I may have had to spend more time on research, but as it was I had lots of notes to refer to, about what I had learnt and who I had learnt it from.

Key Takeaways:

- Reading books written at the time when your story is set provides great background information.

- Take careful notes. There is nothing worse than knowing you have researched something only to then wonder where you found it.

- Take care not to include research findings just for the sake of it. So much time is spent researching that it is tempting to include everything. However, if it does not serve the story then it must be left out.

- Know when to stop researching and start writing. Research can lead down many rabbit holes, but once the bones of the story are there, it is time to start writing. Further research can be done as the need arises.

- Journalling can be a great source of content for non-fiction/memoir writing.

Part 3: Writing the Books

Boughyards Press

Finding My Feet as a Novelist

Conflict at Hanging Rock

I found very early on that I am what is known in the trade as an underwriter. That is, I struggle to get up to the required word count. It is still a mystery to me how other authors can write over 100,000 words and sometimes many more. But then those authors often have the opposite problem, that their manuscripts are too long and they have to cut words. I don't know which would be worse, but I do envy someone who is at least able to get to the required word count. After lots of hard work, I got the bones of the story for *Conflict at Hanging Rock* complete, but I only had 48,000 words. This was just not enough. Normally an historical fiction novel would be at least 80,000 words.

At this point, I decided to pause and put it in the "bottom drawer" for a while until I could get some distance from it. I hoped I could then see where I needed to add more.

In the meantime, I decided to try to start writing something else – another piece of advice from my courses was to rest the current work in progress and write something else. But what to start? So many ideas, none of which seemed perfect. Which one should I choose? I started work on three new projects, none of which ended up being my next manuscript.

I didn't look at my first draft again for about six weeks. Some authors would recommend a longer time, but frankly, I was dying to drag it out again and see if I could make it better; and hopefully longer. I took a deep breath and opened it up. I was pleasantly surprised that it didn't seem nearly as bad as I had thought. I even had a couple of moments when I doubted I had in fact written parts of it because they seemed pretty good.

I decided to print out my draft to start the editing process on paper. My first task was to export it to Microsoft Word from Scrivener which is the writing program I use. That was easy enough, but then I felt trepidation about the next steps. I did not know how to edit, despite all the courses I had taken up to this point.

Nevertheless, I bravely took my flash drive to Officeworks to print a copy and nervously tried to look at it as a reader. Sometimes as a writer, it is difficult to assess your work as a reader would. I made many notes on that first printout, with my newly purchased red pen. It seemed to be much easier to edit the printed copy. I then made these edits in Microsoft Word and repeated the process. After one more time the third print copy had far fewer red marks than the first, so I reckoned I was getting closer. Finally, after several more read throughs and a bit more tinkering, I decided I had done as much as I could without some feedback. I had added some words, even though I had deleted plenty as well, but it was still not nearly long enough. I hoped that my beta readers and editor would have some ideas for additions to the story.

When I decided that I had done everything I could with my first manuscript, I knew it was time for someone else to read my work. The thought of this step was daunting, but it really shouldn't have been that hard. After all, I had been sharing short stories on my blog for years.

But I needed to find a beta reader I could trust. Trust was a huge issue for me when I first shared my work. Beta readers also need to provide useful feedback. At that stage, I didn't have a network of authors whom I could ask. I approached my niece who is an avid reader and a person I knew I could trust. She had never been a beta reader before, and it was hard to know whether she would be able to tell me where my story lacked substance or where it was boring or confusing. Not because of lack of ability but because she might not want to dampen my spirits. I needed to give her some guidance.

A quick internet search revealed lots of examples of questions to assist beta readers in providing worthwhile feedback. With the help of these suggestions, I developed a set of questions to give her some idea of the comments I wanted her to make. I sent them off to her together with the manuscript. I was obviously hoping for more than "Yes, it is fabulous." She didn't disappoint me. She had obviously put a lot of thought into her responses. I was extremely grateful to her, and I found that her ideas for improvement were incredibly useful. She answered all the questions thoroughly, and I implemented quite a few of her suggestions. She even mentioned a few things that the professional editor mentioned later. I still smile to myself at her comment about how often I used the word beautiful to describe the women in the book. She was absolutely right. When I ran a find in the software, I was more than a little surprised by how often I used the word. It's funny that, to this day, I still pull myself up when describing anything as beautiful. Surely I should be able to come up with other words to describe the strong, vibrant women in my stories. It still makes me cringe when I go to use that word as I realise I use it quite a lot in my normal conversation.

Beta readers are fabulous. I am incredibly grateful to these people who commit so much time and thought to providing feedback. It is no small thing. And recently I have been able to reciprocate by being a beta reader for others which also helps my own writing.

Once I had made changes based on my beta reader's suggestions and run the manuscript through a spelling and grammar checker, it was time to employ the services of a professional editor. When it came time to find an editor, I did a search and found the Freelance Editors Network. There was an editor listed on the website who lived in Woodend, close to where my first book is set. This seemed a good omen, so I sent her an email.

She wasn't able to help but gave me some useful feedback after I sent her a sample of my manuscript.

At the same time, I posted on Instagram, and a friend recommended an editor that she knew. I contacted her and was pleased when she responded quickly and seemed keen to do the job. She was very professional and sent a quote. It was more expensive than I had expected, but what did I know? I thought it sounded like a thorough editing proposal, and she could start pretty much immediately. So we entered into an agreement.

By this stage, I knew enough to know that whilst I felt I had done as much as I could, it was nowhere near ready yet. But I also knew I had to take the plunge and get a professional to look at it because by now I couldn't see the forest for the trees. I was so familiar with the story that I couldn't see any way to make it better.

The first step was to make sure my manuscript was ready to be sent. I made some formatting changes to make it more readable. When I did eventually send it, I mentioned I was still not thrilled with it, especially not with the ending.

She had the manuscript back to me quite quickly, with lots of suggestions, some of which included "killing my darlings." Authors will be very familiar with this term. It refers to the practice of cutting that piece of your manuscript that you think is amazing, but your editor is telling you is not working for one reason or another. Mind you, I didn't throw out any of the bits that I cut. I still have the original version of the manuscript, thinking that maybe those great bits that I cut would come in handy one day for some other piece of work. Of course, I haven't even thought about digging out those darlings at any time since. I doubt I ever will.

I soon came to realise that I still had a long way to go. When I first opened the email and read my editor's suggestions, I was completely overwhelmed. I didn't know what to think. It felt like she was suggesting a complete rewrite. Luckily though, through listening to hours of podcasts, I had heard plenty of authors say that they often experienced the same feelings of despair when they first looked at edits. Their advice was to let it sit for a little while to sink in, and then it would not seem as bad. That is exactly what I did.

It certainly wasn't that I didn't agree with nearly all the suggestions she made, it was just that I did not know how I was going to implement the changes. After allowing some time to digest her suggestions, we met in an online meeting and talked them through, which clarified what I needed to do. Yes, there was still a lot of work to do, but it wasn't as bad as I had first thought.

I went back to the drawing board, working hard on it for about eight weeks. The last step in this stage of the edit was to run it through the spell checker again. Once again, I was a little surprised at the number of corrections I had to make. I was glad that I hadn't given in to the little voice that was telling me I didn't need to complete this step again. It certainly was worth the extra hour it took to run it through again.

Back to the editor it went for the second round. In all, there were three rounds. Each time I thought I must be close this time, but back it would come with lots more changes to be made. Eventually we were both reasonably happy with the manuscript.

I had added more to the story during the editing process, and eventually it finished up at 55,600 words. Slightly longer than a novella but still too short. I knew this would not be considered enough for a historical fiction novel by most publishers. I know that the manuscript could have more character development and more descriptive passages about the setting but just getting that many words down and edited seemed like a minor miracle to me. The length of this manuscript is one of several reasons I didn't even attempt to find a traditional publisher. But I just could not seem to find any way to increase the content. This probably means I should not have published the book. However, I was keen to get it out into the world, so I went ahead and self-published it, finished or not.

Why was I particularly determined to get this book out into the world? Simple! I wanted to say I had published a book and to hold it in my hand. The fact that it was not a literary masterpiece was not as important to me as telling the story. Fortunately, I am in a privileged position in that I didn't need it to make money. This was an important consideration for me as an author. I needed to decide what my goal was for my first book, which was to see this story in print. It is a story from my family history, which has fascinated me for many years. I was determined to bring it to fruition.

That's the story of how *Conflict at Hanging Rock* was made. But I had a lot more stories to tell. Whilst I was going through the throes of publishing the book, I started on my next manuscript.

Key Takeaways:

- Putting the manuscript away for a period of time can help to gain some distance from the story and allow you to realise it is not all bad.

- A good beta reader is worth their weight in gold.

- Learn not to let the overwhelm take over when first reading edits.

- Determination and persistence can get you through to the publication of the story you badly want to tell.

Writing with Courage

Breaking Free

After a lot of procrastination and deep thinking, another idea fell into my lap. Once again, reading *Searching for Charlotte* inspired me and reminded me that history has erased many women's stories.

Women are missing from many of the records. This continued in some ways until quite recently. It surprised me to learn that even in 1980, female winners at the Wimbledon Tennis Grand Slam were known by their husbands' names. To this day, Evonne Goolagong is listed on the winners board as Mrs R. A. Cawley. Until 2019, the scoreboards even announced whether they were Miss or Mrs. The men, of course, did not have Mr before their names.

But back in the 1800s, women had even less agency. If they were married, they could not even own property. Everything belonged to their husbands. However, there seem to have been many strong businesswomen who somehow found their way around some of these draconian regulations. Their stories are buried slightly deeper in the annals of history.

I decided I wanted to base my second manuscript around a strong female character. That was when I found the record of my great-grandmother, who had been incarcerated in Kew Lunatic Asylum.

This record immediately set my imagination racing. I wondered what constituted religious excitement. And further, I wondered what had caused her condition to change so markedly from excited and violent to dull and stupid. I could only assume that drugs were involved in her treatment. So many questions. Despite this dire report, she found her way out of the asylum after only seven months, and four years later she was married. She went on to raise eight children, one of them my grandmother. I decided the next project had to be a story inspired by Clara, portraying the strength and resilience she must have possessed to get on with her life after her time in an institution.

What courage she must have had not only to survive that traumatic experience but to be released after only seven months. Many never escaped the depravity of the asylums of those times. I questioned what had caused her to be committed and how she had managed to be released. This sounded like an intriguing story of a resilient woman that needed to be told, so this is the one I wrote next. Hence, *Breaking Free* was born.

Writing this story differed greatly from my first book because I had much less factual information about my female protagonist. Interestingly, I found a very extensive obituary of her father in the newspapers. But the information about her was much sparser. I had to make a lot of assumptions and build the story around social history, including the way people were treated in asylums in the 1800s and the ways of the Catholic Church of the time. Whilst I had little information about her, I had the usual facts that researching family history unearths, such as births, deaths, marriages and locations. I was careful to stick as closely as possible to these timelines and the knowledge that I did have.

I followed a similar process when editing my second book as I had for the first. I had done a bit of editing as I went, so I felt I had a reasonably solid first draft when I printed it out. It didn't need as many self-editing passes. There were not nearly as many printed versions. By now, as I learned more about editing, I was also starting to think that I could do a lot of the editing straight into the document, rather than printing out so many copies.

When I had done many drafts and was starting to think I was close to the end of the editing process, I attended a webinar presented by Jennie Nash from the Author Accelerator. She talked about her Inside Outline. The process requires giving each chapter a name, then writing a sentence about each of:

Plot - what is the main plot point of the chapter/scene?

Point - what is the point of this part of the plot?

And because of that... what happens? Ask this question to make sure the scene has a purpose.

This process for the entire manuscript should be no more than three pages long. After the webinar I purchased her book and decided to give it a try. I found that, even at that late stage in my editing process, it was still incredibly useful.

My niece was my beta reader once again and gave useful feedback, which I was able to incorporate. By this time, I was developing some connections with other authors, but I still didn't know anyone well enough to ask them to read my early manuscript.

Once I was reasonably happy, it was off to the editor. After editing, this book ended up being a little longer than my first at just under 65,000 words, which was a slight improvement. I felt that the editing was easier this time. The reason for this feeling is not entirely clear, but I hoped it was because I had improved as a writer. I still felt a sense of despair when the edits first arrived, but at least the changes didn't seem to be so extensive. Another reason why this edit might have been easier is that I think this story had a better basic structure. It has a shorter time frame with lots more backstory. I should have learned from that and given my next book a tighter time frame. But unfortunately, I didn't learn from my mistakes in this case. My next book spans nearly 100 years!

Key Takeaways:

- It occurred to me that I wanted to write women's stories to redress the way they had been largely erased from history.

- Scant records can add much to the story if you question them closely.

- Everyone's process is different. Editing as I write works for me but for others it might prevent them ever finishing a first draft.

- A shorter time frame for the setting of a book possibly makes it easier to write.

A Story with Wider Horizons

Family & Fortune

My great-great-great-grandmother, who married a convict and travelled with him to Australia in the 1850s, is the inspiration for my third and most recent novel, *Family & Fortune*. Another brave and strong woman. This branch of the family is one I have researched much more recently as they were not well known to myself or my family. My grandfather was adopted, and this is his biological family, who were discovered more recently. The book opens in Bedfordshire, in England, and moves to the goldfields of Castlemaine. But this story contains a mystery. How did these two meet, given that Mary Ann was only 10 years old when Richard was convicted of larceny and sent to Van Diemen's Land? It does not seem likely that their families were known to each other as they lived 100 miles apart, which was quite a distance in those times. And yet Richard, having served his sentence, returned home to England to marry his bride. I had to use my imagination to decide how this meeting might have occurred.

This book was a more ambitious project, and I was determined to achieve my goal of 80,000 words.

I started planning and researching in August 2023, as I was preparing for the launch of *Breaking Free*. There was still a lot of work to do before that launch, which was to be on my birthday, November 13, 2023. But I was itching to make a start on the shiny new idea that had been brewing in my head.

In November every year, writers from all over the world used to join in a challenge to write 50,000 words in NaNoWriMo, which stands for National Novel Writing Month. That's 1,667 words per day; every single day. Quite a lofty goal by anyone's measure. As the month of November approached in 2023, our Write Squad Community decided to take up the challenge. I didn't want to miss out on being a part of it with my new community. But when I looked at all the events on my calendar, I knew that 50,000 words was completely out of the question. I set a much more realistic goal of 20,000 words. That's around 666 words a day if I wrote every day, which is something I don't normally do.

In order to achieve that goal, I knew I would need to have done a lot of research and thinking about the project so the words would flow somewhat easily. Given that I had been researching and planning since August, I had a fair idea of how the novel was going to unfold. I had also written just over 4000 words, so I had something to start with. Often, starting is the hardest part.

I am pleased to say that I achieved that goal. It was a great feeling to have those 20,000 words added to my manuscript in one short month. Especially as I was under a lot of pressure at that time as I also had to launch and market *Breaking Free*.

Of course, the manuscript took me substantially longer to finish even though I had a good start.

With this book, my editing changed quite a bit. I did a lot straight into the manuscript rather than printing it out. When I tried to edit the first printed copy I found it difficult and confusing to make the larger structural edits. It felt easier to correct some of the big issues, typing the changes as I went. There was another benefit of this because it allowed me to continue to work in Scrivener with more ease if I didn't need to print it out. To ensure that I wasn't losing anything critical in the edits, I saved a Word copy each day. It is a simple task to compile a Word document from Scrivener. This is another example of how my process changes with every new project.

Once I had completed the major self-editing it was time to send the manuscript first to my beta readers and then to my editor. At this stage, I exported the document out of Scrivener and started editing straight into the Word document, saving the file with a new name and date each time I changed it. I ended up with about ten versions, not exactly ten additional full edits but ten versions that had substantial differences based on beta reader and editor feedback.

Five months after completing those first 20,000 words in NaNoWriMo, I sent just over 73,000 words to beta readers. By now I had a network of writer friends and felt more confident about sharing my work. I asked my connections if anyone would be willing to read my manuscript. For this book, I had four marvellous beta readers who all gave useful feedback. Once again, I cannot stress enough, how grateful I am for the time they committed to this task.

When the feedback came in, there was another round of self-editing before I would consider sending to my professional editor.

With this book, I tried a different approach to the editing. Many authors have a different editor for each step. There are three main stages of editing. The developmental or structural edit looks at the big picture. The copy edit goes more granular to a line by line edit looking for repetition and inconsistencies. Finally there is the proofread, which picks up spelling and grammar errors. I decided I should give this a try. I employed the services of a developmental editor whom I had come into contact with through my writer network. She had a very different style from my original editor. This added to the overwhelm when I first received her edits. But she taught me so much, which was of tremendous benefit. After I had actioned that round of edits, I was ready for the copy edit, which was done by my original editor.

I had to delete something like 10,000 words from this third manuscript during the editing process. Whilst I hadn't really counted the deleted words in my previous manuscripts, I don't think I had deleted anywhere near that many in either of my other two books. By the time this book was finished, including all the deleted words, and having added many new words, I had written well over my goal word count, but the book finished up being just short of 80,000 words.

Whilst editing hasn't gotten any easier, once I overcome the anxiety that invariably plagues me on first seeing the suggested edits, I do find it an enjoyable part of the process, and I am extremely aware of how much better it makes my books.

Key Takeaways:

- Writing every day is hard but not impossible, at least for a set period of time.

- Editing electronically worked for this manuscript. It might not next time given that my process seems to be different every time.

- Having more than one editor was a great learning experience.

My First Non-fiction

Becoming an Indie Author

This book is my first attempt at writing non-fiction and writing it was quite different from my historical fiction. I needed to inject something of myself into it which I found rather difficult being somewhat of an introvert. But there are also similarities in that my fiction is based on real events and this is also based on real events that I have recorded as I wrote my books.

When I started keeping notes the purpose was to have them to refer back to when I published each new book. With over twelve months between the publication of each novel, I found it hard to remember all the processes for self-publishing. It proved a useful strategy. But I soon began to wonder whether all my random notes and the ups and downs of the process might be of interest to others. That was when I decided to attempt to write a non-fiction book.

As I went through the process, I experienced the usual self-doubt, questioning my decision to move away from historical fiction. After all, who was I to be giving advice to other writers. Another of my doubts centred on my usual issue of reaching a decent word count. This book is only about 40,000 words. But I don't think that is such an issue with a book of this type. I think the work is complete and I have said everything I wanted to say.

Once I had done several passes to self-edit my work it was again time for beta readers. I had recently done a beta read for another historical fiction author and so I asked her if she would like to return the favour. I was pleased when she agreed. Her feedback made me feel a lot better about the work as I had been having a bit of a crisis of confidence about it at that point.

As this book included a lot of my experiences with self-publishing, I wanted to ask some other self-published authors if they would be willing to read it and provide feedback. Two generous authors whom I have connected with recently agreed. They also gave me positive and useful feedback. I was incredibly pleased that early readers responded positively and seemed to find it valuable.

Once I had made changes based on the suggestions of these readers the manuscript was off to my editor again. What a delightful surprise it was when she sent me an update to say that she thought the book was great. Such a huge relief. Then when the edits came back, for the first time I did not need to freak out at all. She informed me that the edits needed were minor, and that she had really enjoyed reading it. But there was one editing lesson I wish I had remembered earlier.

Keeping my journal not only proved useful in the self-publishing process but also when I was going through self-editing. As I edited each book I referred back to some of my notes to remind myself of the things I particularly needed to check. In fact, I should have referred to them more closely when first editing this book. My editor was able to inform me that I had used the word really 75 times, actually 30 times and definitely 24 times. When I did refer back to my editing notes I found that one thing on my editing checklist was to do a search for over used words.

Key Takeaways:

- Moving away from a genre you are experienced in can be daunting.

- Self-doubt is ever present.

- An editing checklist is a useful tool.

Plotter or Pantser

In author terminology, writers are said to be either plotters or pantsers, that is they either carefully plot everything out before commencing the writing or they "fly by the seat of their pants" and just see where the story takes them. Some authors don't like the term "pantser" and would prefer to be called discovery writers, which I do think is a much better term. Discovery writers feel they lose some of the fun of writing if they know exactly where the story is going. But on the other hand, many authors are meticulous plotters who know almost exactly what the story will be before they begin writing.

Personally, from what I have read and heard, I am of the opinion that all authors must have some idea of a plot, even if it is not on paper, before they start writing, and even the most determined plotter will go off track and let the characters take them where they will. My feeling is that all authors are probably a mix of the two, in varying degrees. Interestingly, in her novel ***Save the Cat! Writes a Novel***, which refers to a story structure with three acts and further subdivided into fifteen beats, Jessica Brody maintains that we all have to plot at some stage. Pantsers will need to do this after the first draft, whereas plotters do it before beginning writing. She believes that the structure has to be added to the story at some point.

I am still unsure whether I would classify myself as a plotter or a pantser. Each book so far has used a different writing process. I wonder if the reason I struggle such a lot with structure is because I write family stories that often span long time frames, and I find it difficult to fit them into a three-act structure. I tried using the *Save the Cat* structure, but I found it far too constricting for my stories. I am working as closely as possible to a three act structure making sure that the characters have an arc which shows how they change by the end of the book and that there is an inciting incident which upsets the status quo at the beginning of the book. I try to ensure that there is a climax somewhere near the end and that the books finish with all the plot lines satisfactorily tied up. I think that if I can include all these facets in my stories, then I have enough structure.

Conflict at Hanging Rock

With my first book, I did little actual plotting. But I did do a lot of research and thinking before I started writing. Because my stories are based on fact, I always have a timeline that I try to adhere to. I definitely add my ideas of how events might have unfolded to make the story more engaging, but it is important to me not to change the facts as I know them. My writing was not done in a linear fashion in this book. I wrote all over the place. When I felt stuck with one chapter, I would move to a scene or chapter that I felt ready to write, in order to just get the words down. This makes for an extremely messy first draft. I know the first draft is supposed to be messy, but this was particularly chaotic. I think if I had done more planning, the editing stage would have been easier. And perhaps I would have been able to make the story longer.

Breaking Free

I was learning all the time, and so my plan for this manuscript was to do lots of research and plot this story out in much greater detail than I had done previously before starting to write. I tried a couple of different methods, including writing a comprehensive outline and using index cards. Once again I had a timeline with dates and places, and the report from the Asylum but not a lot of anything else. I fleshed out my timeline, adding in some of the historical events that were happening at that time, whether I intended them to be incorporated in my story or not. Even so, there were many inclusions in the book that cropped up as I wrote. For example, one theme in particular that I hadn't intended to include was the Women's Franchise Movement. This came about after my editor suggested that I give the character of the matron of the asylum a larger part in the story. She became an activist working for women's rights.

I also fleshed out my characters a lot more before starting to write. By the time I started, I felt quite close to Annie, and also to her father. I think it is a better book because of this process, and it is also longer, with the final word count coming in at 64,000 words, but still well short of my 80,000 word goal.

Family & Fortune

When I started writing my third book, I was still none the wiser about the best process for me. I had continued reading, listening and learning, and the more I learnt, the more I felt I had to come up with my own process. As I wrote this book, I thought my process was somewhere in the middle. Somewhere between a plotter and a discovery writer. Some planning and some winging it. But I was still focused on learning more about the writing craft. I was able to find a lot of information about this branch of my ancestors, so this novel once again contains quite a lot of factual content. I think my character development has continued to improve in the writing of this novel, and this time I got enticingly close to reaching my goal of 80,000 words. The book went to print with 79,600 words.

Becoming an Indie Author

In the writing of this book, which is my first non-fiction manuscript, I did little plotting. But this is a very different book. As I was writing my first novel, I started making notes about everything I was discovering and learning about writing and self-publishing. All of those notes became this book. I don't think it would have been possible to plot before I began because I didn't know what I didn't know.

But now, after completing and publishing four books, I still don't know whether I work better as a plotter or a discovery writer. I am generally a fairly organised person, so it stands to reason that as I develop my writing craft and learn more about how to plot and the tools to use, I will become more of a plotter. Whilst I will work on plotting from now on, I will always let the story take me where it will. I don't know all the facts about my ancestors, so as I write I need to use my imagination to fill in the blanks. I think this is where the discovery part comes in. There are merits in the discovery writing process as well.

Key Takeaways:

- One thing that is clear now is that the process for every book is different.

- The writing process seems to be different for every author. There is no right or wrong way. It is more about what works for the individual.

- Plotting or Discovery writing are both legitimate processes.

Part 4: Becoming an Author

Boughyards Press

Building a Writing Routine

Writing is hard work. This fact cannot be understated. I often struggle to get more than a couple of hundred words on the page in one sitting. Occasionally it flows easily, but it is the times it doesn't that really put a writer off.

One thing is clear, and that is that writing needs to become a habit. Whilst I am writing the first draft, I need to turn up, perhaps not every day but certainly on a regular basis. I find I lose track of my plot and characters if I leave it too long between sessions. I need to have some structure. Although I do find it beneficial to occasionally let the story sit for a while until inspiration strikes. Thinking time to me is just as important as writing time.

When I first began writing, I was still working full time in a challenging role. To make my writing a habit and to achieve the goals I had set myself to become a published author, I needed to put some things in place.

I am definitely a morning person. Whilst doing the Diploma of Family History, I had been getting up every morning at 5:30 for the two years it took to complete the course, so I had already developed that habit. When I began writing my first book, I continued that practice. To assist with the early morning starts, I go to bed around 8:30pm and read for a while before falling asleep.

After I retired from my full-time job, I continued to work in the same industry for about 15 hours a week. Realistically, that meant I should have had plenty of time to write. Well, no, it wasn't actually that easy. Work may have only formally been fifteen hours per week, but there were so many other administrative things that came along that didn't quite fit into paid work time. Fifteen hours doesn't sound like a lot, but together with some other rather intense family responsibilities, including taking over most of the household tasks, it didn't leave a lot of time for writing.

A couple of years ago, I decided I needed to take life a bit easier as I was feeling stressed. I gave up part of my day job and promised myself I would say no to all other offers of work. Well, that didn't quite work out the way I hoped. I also have a problem with saying no to work that takes my interest.

The work I had been doing was on projects that really stimulated me and allowed me to stay more connected with people. And I am not exactly complaining because the external work subsidised what is still an expensive writing hobby. No, writing is not making me any money yet. But my current financial position allows me to support my writing without the need for the other work. My next major goal was to finish up all external work, which was not writing related, by the end of 2025. I am pleased to say I learnt to say no, and have not accepted any new projects in 2026.

It is not even just about writing time. There is the learning – so much learning. First, it was learning to write. Then, when I decided to self-publish, I had another round of learning, and of course marketing and promotion also became a priority. In fact, the learning never ends.

I don't write every day. When I am in the throes of the publishing process, for example, I have learnt that I need to give it most of my attention. There is so much to do and a lot of mental power required. I don't beat myself up if I am not writing much during that phase. I know I am still working on my writing, just at a different stage of the process.

I keep a notebook to help me see exactly what I have achieved each day, that might be a word count, pages of editing or some of the myriad tasks to get ready for publishing, It keeps me on track and provides me with motivation when I can see at a glance what I have achieved in a particular week.

My writing includes more than just the manuscript I am working on at a particular time, too. I write a blog post, a newsletter every month and my journal. Recently I have also joined Substack, which is a subscription based platform where creators can publish content and build communities. I am now releasing a newsletter on that platform as well. I figure all the words count no matter where I write them.

There are other writing projects I try to fit in. I am learning how to write engaging short stories. I have also taken part in the writing challenges presented by my Diploma alumni writing group. They are short stories, usually less than 1000 words. This is great practice and a break from work on the current project, which I sometimes find can be beneficial.

For the moment though, I would like to write for at least 30 minutes, five days a week. That does not sound like a lot, but I can often write about 500 words in that time, which is better than nothing. Of course, this doesn't happen every day as life gets in the way. Some days my word count is next to nothing. Some days, of course, I get on a roll and work for quite a bit longer. But an undemanding and achievable goal such as this also allows time for plotting the next book or attending to administrative tasks, which, as a self-published author, take a lot of time. A self-published author should divide the workload 50/50. Half for writing and half for administrative tasks. I try to write in the morning and then do the other tasks in the afternoon, fitting my other work in around this schedule.

As I am supposed to be retired, or at least semi-retired, I decided a while ago, to start the day more gently by spending an hour reading in bed with a coffee rather than racing out of bed at 5:30 to start writing. It has proven to be a fantastic decision. I love reading, and this change led to my reading 63 books in 2024 and another 60 in 2025. Of course, an author considers reading to be work. We learn such a lot from other authors. I never feel guilty about my reading time.

As I contemplated my fourth historical fiction manuscript, November 2024 was approaching. That meant considering taking part in NaNoWriMo again. I decided I was nowhere near ready to write yet, having not done nearly enough planning and research on the work I was going to begin next. *Family & Fortune* was still being edited and made ready for publishing, so I decided not to do NaNoWriMo. But then the Write Squad Community decided to have a separate challenge to write 500 words a day. Once again, I didn't want to miss out. This was not the greatest decision as I was nowhere near well enough prepared. But despite my lack of preparation, I managed to write 500 words each day. Now there is a dreadfully messy manuscript with 15,000 words, which covers the entire story that I want to write eventually. Since some authors write outlines of this length, I suppose I could consider this an outline. As I write now, in 2026, that manuscript is still waiting for me to get back to it. Although it is a messy first draft, at least they are words, which have made me think the story through. When I get back to it, I will probably need to rewrite a lot of it. But if I had not committed to writing 500 words per day, I would not have the beginnings of another novel and, as they say, you can't edit a blank page.

I am not sure I would ever commit to the NaNoWriMo 50,000 word goal – it seems unachievable. But that is a moot point now. Recently, after several years of financial instability and some other issues, NaNoWriMo is no more. Sad but true. But November was never great timing for those of us in the Southern Hemisphere anyway. Our weather is warming up, and we want to be outside more, not to mention the busyness of the end of the year and preparation for the festive season and summer holidays. There are a couple of other similar programs which started in November last year. We will see where they go.

But in the meantime, I can set my own goals and do my own thing without the need for programs such as NaNoWriMo. I am a goal-driven person, and if I say I am going to do something, I mostly get it done. I recently set a goal to have this manuscript to my editor by a specific date, giving myself a deadline. I am pleased to say I achieved that goal.

Key Takeaways:

- Writing needs to become a habit.

- Find the time of day that works best for you.

- Let the process evolve and change as the need arises.

- Juggling making a living to pay the bills and getting the words written can be a difficult balance.

Dealing with Self-doubt

All writers talk about imposter syndrome. I don't know any writers who haven't experienced it. Statistics tell us that nearly 7 in 10 people will struggle with feeling like an imposter at some time. Among authors and creators, it is likely to be more like 9 in 10. Even the best authors experience it, which seems to me to indicate that it isn't a sign of incompetence, but a result of wanting to aim high.

I have definitely experienced this self-doubt. When I first started writing, doubt was a constant companion. There is always a voice whispering in my ear, "Your writing is not good enough," "You will never be as good as [insert favourite author here]." Whenever I read a brilliant novel, I wonder why I bother writing at all.

Michael Robotham, a superb Australian crime writer who has written many outstanding books, says that when he sends his final manuscript to his agent, he always signs off with the words "we fooled them again".

As a self-published author, I don't need to 'fool' an agent or publisher. But that also means I don't have the validation that comes with having my work accepted by a publisher, which of course adds to the self-doubt.

I don't set out to achieve literary excellence, but I do want to believe that each book I write is better than the last because with each book I learn more about the craft of writing.

Everyone says that if you want to be a writer, all you really need to do is write. But what about becoming an author? Is there a difference? Looking at the dictionary definitions of both words, this is what I found.

The *Cambridge English Dictionary* defines a writer as:

- someone who writes books or articles to be published.

The definition of an author is:

- a writer of a book, article, etc., or a person whose primary job it is to write books.

Some might give an answer more along the lines that a writer is someone who writes, whilst an author is someone who has writing published. I decided I wanted to become an author whilst continuing to be a writer.

I could not see how I would ever overcome imposter syndrome. In the end, I recognised it is a common pattern in a writer's life, not a reflection of my actual ability. When my doubting self whispers that I am not good enough, I write anyway. Networking with other writers has helped me to understand that I was not alone in feeling inadequate. The fact that most authors experience imposter syndrome is quite comforting somehow. Instead of thinking thoughts like, 'I am not a proper writer,' I tell myself, 'I write, therefore I am a writer'.

When I reached 25,000 words in my first book, I came to a huge roadblock. For me, it felt like such an accomplishment to get this far. But I knew I still had a long way to go. Where was I going to get another 25,000 words, let alone the additional 55,000 words, that I was aiming for? What if I couldn't finish this book that I had sweated over for so long? I had told everyone I was going to write a book. What if I simply couldn't do it? It just didn't bear thinking about. I remember feeling so overwhelmed that, on many occasions, I was afraid to open my file. It might seem ridiculous. I wasn't going to die, but it was a genuine fear. I actually felt physically ill.

I had the same problem with my second and third manuscripts of not being able to write enough words. I was more accepting of it though as I knew I had written a book, and that with persistence, I could do it again. I was pleased that each of my novels ended up being a little longer than the last, until with my third manuscript I almost made it to my goal of 80,000 words.

Despite all the doubts and misgivings, I somehow eventually manage to get a messy first draft finished each time. Many authors say that the first draft is the toughest part. That you just need to get it done. It will be messy but that is completely okay. Once the first draft is done it can be edited, but you can't edit a blank page There is a lot of wisdom in these statements. But the doubts continue through the self-editing process, as I question how many drafts I need to write. I continually ask myself, is it ready yet? Am I just being too pedantic?

When I finally decide that I can prolong the agony no more, the time comes to allow someone else to read my work. The thought of doing that is possibly scarier than that awful roadblock when I reached 25,000 words in my first book. I think this is perhaps the most anxiety inducing time of all. Up to this point, I was the only person who had read my work. But now I had to acknowledge that I wanted others to read it as well. I need not have worried because, without exception, the beta readers I have trusted with my work have been kind, providing thoughtful feedback. And the same must be said of my professional editors.

Once I had implemented all the feedback and felt that there were no further improvements that I could make, I was ready to face the next fear. I could not believe how stressed I felt at taking the irrevocable step to publish my books and put my work out into the world. This step is always a huge deal when I fully commit to allowing anyone who would like to read my book to do so, rather than just those I have chosen to allow to read it. No longer do I have the ability to decide who I would trust with my work. I could get dreadful reviews, and I would either have to not read them or deal with my feelings about them. I didn't think my work was that bad, so I don't know why I was so anxious. One of my major worries with the first book was that it was only 200 pages. But the three people who had read it early on, seemed to think it was pretty good, and only one of them commented on the length. It was a relief that my other two books ended up closer to an adequate length.

Having said all this, could my first completed manuscript really be worth publishing? Well, maybe it wasn't. Many authors will tell you they have several discarded manuscripts languishing in the proverbial bottom drawer. I simply couldn't do that with this thing that I had worked so hard on for years. As I have already mentioned, the story was too important to me, and I wanted it to be read.

On the other hand, there are many acclaimed debut novels that reach the market every day and sell a good number of books. I thought, why couldn't that be my novel? The very next thought was much less positive. What makes me think I have the knowledge and skills to write a book – any book? Could I become a published author? I was not at all sure I could pursue this slightly crazy goal. Whilst I have written many words over the course of my 60-plus years, does any of that qualify me to be a writer, to publish a book? I thought the answer to that question was a hard no. Although I suppose all my previous writing had been good practice, I soon discovered that writing a book is such a different beast to anything else I had ever written.

I couldn't let fear take over. I had to push down my anxiety and upload my precious work and hope I didn't get too many terrible reviews. One thing that provides the most trepidation when launching a book is what people are going to think of it. Family and friends are often complimentary, but what about total strangers? In reality, the books were probably more likely not to get noticed at all, which is pretty much how it has turned out. I have only a handful of reviews on any of my books, but happily there is only one bad one so far.

Another source of anxiety is when the book is finally ready and uploaded to all the retail sites and I need to promote it. Just because a book is available, it doesn't mean that anyone is going to purchase it. I, like many authors, am somewhat of an introvert, so talking about myself and asking people to buy my book was always going to be difficult. My first author talk for each of my books was at my local library, where I knew the librarians and I felt quite at home. However, facing the around thirty people who turned up to hear my talk was quite daunting. Interestingly, once the initial nervousness was over, and the talk was underway, I relaxed quickly. Doing the actual talks was not that bad. The hardest thing about promoting my books was asking the question. That is, when I had to email libraries to ask if they would host an author talk, post about my books on social media, asking people to buy them. It was all very daunting, and once again I doubted my ability to market myself and my books.

Left unchecked, the Imposter Syndrome mindset can have negative impacts such as missed opportunities, underpricing my work, and holding back my ideas. But with three books now written and published and with a few fans who have read all three, I can be proud of my achievements so far. But that does not mean the impostor syndrome is gone or even that it is less.

Key Takeaways:

- Imposter Syndrome is a constant. I know it will never go away. But it is common to most authors.

- Feel the fear, but do it anyway.

- Each step in the process has its own anxieties.

Learning the Craft

When I first started writing my stories, I just wrote. I knew nothing about character and story arc. And as for publishing, that was a total mystery. Starting out on a writing journey, there is so much to learn. In the process of 'becoming an author', I sought advice from many places.

The Diploma of Family History showed me that there are many ways to write the stories of my ancestors. It gave me a starting point, but I needed to find out more. I started researching and found that there is a lot of expert advice freely available online. Newsletters written by other authors, who generously shared their knowledge, were one substantial source of inspiration. I also began listening to several great podcasts, and whilst some of these come and go, my favourites, at the moment, include **So You Want to Be a Writer**, **Writes 4 Women**, **The Word Count** and **The Creative Penn**. Podcasts are probably still my preferred learning tool as I can listen to them on my morning walk every day. Listening to interviews with published authors provides so much insight about the writing process, and indeed, how different everyone's writing process is. The knowledge gleaned from author interviews gave me the confidence to tread my own path. Whilst there are tried-and-true writing and editing strategies, everyone interprets them a little differently.

My next step was to enrol in some courses at the Australian Writers Centre. I have completed Creative Writing Part 1, Creative Non-Fiction, Historical Fiction and a few others that were motivational tools including Mojo Month, Reinvent Yourself and a course in how to use Scrivener. They were all great courses, and I learnt a lot about writing craft.

Recently I enrolled in Pamela Cook's Turn up the Tension course, another terrific learning experience.

There are many useful books about writing craft available. The first one I read was **So You Want To Be A Writer**, by Valerie Khoo and Allison Tait. I was working full time when I read it, and this book focussed on how to write a book whilst you still have a day job. I found it engaging and incredibly useful.

Next, I read **The Writing Book** by Kate Grenville. I only had a library copy, so I think this is one I need to add to my collection because I would like to explore it further.

Fairly early on, I purchased **Save the Cat Writes a Novel** by Jessica Brody. I have tried many times to fit my stories into this structure with limited success. I think I have almost given up ever completely understanding how to implement such a complex story structure.

Another one is Jennie Nash's book, which is called **Blue-print for a Book**. I tried using what she calls the Inside Outline for plotting. I had some success with it, but I found that, for me, it works better after writing the first draft.

Graeme Simsion's book, **The Novel Project**, details yet another planning and plotting strategy based on The Three-Act Structure but also contains a lot more strategies. I enjoyed the book and used some ideas in it.

I also read Stephen King's excellent book, **On Writing**, which contained yet another set of ideas. Interestingly, the first time I read *On Writing*, I wasn't sure how useful it was for me. However, I read it again more recently and found that I understood the message much more clearly. Perhaps this is not the best book for beginner writers.

Most authors understand that you cannot be a writer without being a reader. Stephen King says, 'If you don't have the time to read, you don't have the time (or the tools) to write. Simple as that.' I agree with this wholeheartedly. I love to read many different genres, and I learn such a lot from what other authors write. Some authors say that they don't read in the genre they are writing in whilst they are writing. Their argument is that they feel like the author's work might influence them and that they might even unknowingly plagiarise. However, I would argue that I want to be inspired and influenced by great authors. Isn't that how we learn? I was pleased to read in **Reading Like a Writer** by Francine Prose, that the author of this book was of the same opinion.

All of these books, courses and podcasts have added something to my knowledge of the writing craft. But face-to-face events have also been a big part of my learning. I had watched interviews online and listened to many podcasts, but it is so exciting and inspirational to attend an event in real life.

Unfortunately, I haven't had many opportunities to attend conferences and festivals but when I do, it is completely worth it. The networking with other like-minded people is worth it alone. I need to add a disclaimer here. Being an introvert, I find these events daunting, and I always end the event feeling totally exhausted, but it is certainly worth the effort.

In May 2022, I attended my first face-to-face writers festival – the Bendigo Writers Festival on the weekend of 13th–15th May.

After travelling from my home town of Yarrawonga to Bendigo, I was excited about my first session. It was a workshop session, so I was looking forward to getting some actual writing done.

Alice Grundy, who is an editor and publisher, delivered the workshop. The topic was 'How to Get Published'.

She took us through the process of writing a one-sentence tagline or hook, a bio and also a synopsis. We could volunteer to read our work out loud to the group, and Alice gave some feedback, although quite brief. I took the opportunity to read out my one-line hook, which put me well outside my comfort zone.

Between each of the writing exercises, she gave us some publishing tips. And whilst a lot of this was useful information, I would have preferred more input from Alice about what we should be writing in each exercise. She gave some instructions, but they were also brief.

Most of her information was about traditional publishing, and she only briefly touched on self-publishing. She said there was not as much stigma as there used to be.

The next session I attended was 'Do Books Matter' with David Henley, Cath Moore and Terri-ann White. The facilitator was Gemma Rayner. David and Terri-ann are both publishers, and Cath is an author.

They talked about what would be published and what wouldn't. And about the merits of e-books and audiobooks.

The next session I attended was 'Friends' with Kate Mildenhall and Karen Viggers. This was a very interesting discussion between two people who are obviously friends themselves. At the time Kate had a podcast with her friend Katherine Collette called *The First Time*. Now I love podcasts, but I had been avoiding adding any more to my ridiculously long list. However, I knew I had to listen to this one as Kate is such an engaging person. Karen and Kate mentioned many books about friendship. At the time, I thought how good it would be to have more time to get through more of these fabulous titles. Now I am fortunate to have more time, and I have read over 150 books in the last two years. But it doesn't seem to matter how many I read; there are always many more on my list that I long to read.

Unfortunately, the next session I was scheduled to attend was cancelled. It was supposed to be with Graeme Simsion, and the topic was 'How Is It Written'. I was disappointed to miss it but, fortunately, I got to see an online interview with him not long after.

Instead, I went to 'Dare to Fail' with John Marsden and host Pam Snow. This was a fabulous session. John was such an intelligent man who unfortunately passed away recently. He had some challenging ideas. He spoke briefly about the overuse of the word bullying, which I found fascinating. I wish the host had asked him more about that. He also mentioned a conversation he overheard where one speaker said, "Einstein was brilliant because he could think outside the box." The response was, "Ah yes, but to think outside the box, you need to know what's in the box."

I also attended 'Australiana' with Cath Moore, Yumna Kassab and host David Henley. The two women both identify as city girls but had both recently written books that are set in country Australia. Such an interesting discussion about the differences between writing about the country and the city.

The last session of the weekend was 'The Creative Life' with Charlotte Wood and host Karen Viggers. I was reading Charlotte's book, ***The Luminous Solution***, which is on this topic. It was great to hear Charlotte talk about some of the concepts in the book. The fundamental question was, how do you find the freedom to flourish? I was interested to hear Charlotte mention that walking and the natural world fed her creativity. I hear that from so many authors, and I know a walk on my favourite track by the river will help me think of solutions to plot problems or just generally come up with new ideas.

The entire festival was a fantastic learning experience, which I thoroughly enjoyed.

I attended the Bendigo Writers Festival again in 2023, and once again it was a wonderful experience. But in 2024, the organisers had changed the date, and it clashed with the Romance Writers of Australia (RWA) Conference which I was keen to attend with my niece.

The RWA Conference was held in Adelaide in 2024 at the beautiful seaside suburb of Glenelg. The event began as usual with the fancy dress cocktail party. Newbies like us were invited to attend a special welcoming event prior to the cocktail party.

The first day of the conference saw lots of informative sessions. Not being a romance writer, I wasn't sure how much I would learn and whether I would feel out of place. I certainly did not, as everyone was extremely welcoming.

One of the first sessions I attended was 'Success with Series' presented by Anne Gracie. I have not written a series but hope to do that eventually. There was lots of expert advice, like to write ahead because readers are impatient, so don't like to wait too long for the next in series. Don't make a series too long, 3 or 4 books is appropriate, and don't hold the best for last; write the best first book and try to make each one better. She also alerted me to what has become my favourite series of all time, ***The Seven Sisters*** by Lucinda Reilly.

Another session I attended was titled 'Your Literary Legacy'. I got lots of good tips about how not to leave a mess for your family from that session. I am still working on that.

One reason for attending the event was to find ways to inject more romance into my books. 'Writing Between the Sheets' was a perfect session. The main point I took from that was that sex scenes are not physical; they are emotional. And also, how important it is to write to your own comfort level, be that open or closed door sex scenes. I took many more notes in that session. It was probably my favourite of the conference.

On Saturday night we attended the Gala Awards Dinner, a formal affair with delicious food and drinks and the best company. Some of the Write Squad Community won awards, so it was an exciting event.

But the best part of the entire event was meeting so many friendly writers, including meeting our Write Squad Community friends in real life (IRL) for the first time.

I have also attended many other author events presented by our local library. Amanda Hampson, Kylie Orr, Shelley Burr, Sandie Docker, Fiona McArthur and Kyra Geddes are just some of the authors who have visited.

I had to travel a little further to listen to some other talented authors. My favourite historical fiction author, Darry Fraser, spoke at the Benalla Library twice with her last two books. Of particular interest was Darry's use of props. She had a professional trailer recorded for her book with an actor wearing clothes to match the cover image. That costume, including the incredible hat made by her friend, was on display at her talks. This was such a clever marketing idea.

I travelled a significant distance to meet Holly Brunnbauer, the debut author of ***What Did I Miss?*** in 2025. Holly is also a member of our Write Squad Community. It was lovely to finally meet her. I asked her about the fact that some of her characters had turned out to be not as flawed as I first thought. She reminded me that to be real, characters need to have several sides to their personalities. She also pointed out that in the beginning of the book we were getting to know one of the male characters from the point of view of his ex-wife, which of course was a rather different view than others had of him.

I have also attended talks by Kate Solly, Margaret Hickey, and Chris Hammer at other libraries. Every event was worth the trip.

One of my favorite recent events was the workshop, 'Brief but Brilliant: The art of short storytelling', presented by Anne Freeman. It was such a fun workshop with lots of reminders and new lessons. One thing that particularly resonated with me was that when writing a short story, you need to enter late and exit early, avoiding lengthy setups.

Across the Arts, a local group, also puts on a wonderful bookish event each year with a range of authors who have included Kylie Ladd, Kerryn Mayne, Lisa Ireland, Sally Hepworth and Jane Cockram. We've also had the privilege of hearing Jelena Dokic talk about her books.

During her most recent visit to my home town, Lisa Ireland ran a workshop before her conversation with Kate Solly. It was an incredibly informative workshop with lots of tips but one thing that was a great reminder was remembering the importance of creativity. Why we write is important.

All of these resources and events have made such a difference to my learning and writing journey. Apart from this, I have also had quite a lot of help from my new author friends.

Key Takeaways:

- There is a huge amount of freely available writing craft advice online.

- Have a range of writing craft books on your bookshelf to refer to.

- Accessing online courses and events is worthwhile, but in person events are different and quite special. It is a good idea to take a notebook and pencil to these events because you always learn something.

A Little Help from My Friends

I have found that writers' groups and author networks are incredibly helpful for an emerging author.

Very early in my writing journey, I joined Now Novel. This is a UK community, which offers online writing groups based on certain criteria. One group I joined was for older writers, whilst another was for historical fiction writers. They were extremely active groups, which, from experience, I have found is not always common in online communities of practice. I started to share small sections of my manuscript and found that the members of the group demonstrated skill in providing feedback in a positive and thoughtful way. I got some excellent critiques, which were a great help as I reworked some of my manuscript. They included great suggestions, which I think led to some improvements. In return for receiving these critiques, I was expected to provide critiques for others. I found this a useful skill to develop when I was undertaking the Diploma of Family History. I learnt a lot by critiquing others' work and considering how I thought it could be improved. However, for whatever reason, I let my participation in that community lapse. Perhaps one reason was that it was mostly UK-based writers, and I felt I needed to make some Australian connections.

Then I joined Allison Tait's group, Write With A L Tait. This was my first subscription-based group and it was so helpful at the beginning of my journey. Allison offered lots of expert advice. I met a lot of authors, both well-known and aspiring. It was a great experience. There was a small monthly fee, but this suited me, as I found it much better than having to fork out hundreds of dollars for another course. Allison hosted monthly 'Ask Me Anything' live sessions and interviews with other authors and industry experts.

The people in the group were friendly, and I made some good connections, which I think is one of the best benefits of groups such as this. There was a lot of interaction in the Facebook group. Some of us took part in the Write a Book with Al challenge. Allison posted every day with the number of words she had written, and we all responded with our word count for the day. It was often zero, but that was the same for everyone. It felt good to be able to admit that you had not been able to find time to write in a busy day and there was no judgement. Of course, there was a sense of pride when reporting that the word count for the day was good.

The other challenge was #500in30. The aim of this challenge was for us all to sit down at a particular time set by Allison and try to write 500 words in 30 minutes. Once again there was no pressure, but knowing that I could have a small brag about the number of words I wrote or seek commiserations if I didn't get many words down, was motivational. I could feel the support of the other members.

Allison also generously offered me a guest blog spot on her website. I wrote a piece about writing family history as fiction.

Taking part in that group was one of the best things I have done for my writing practice.

I eventually moved on from this group and took up another paid subscription, which was Jane Friedman's newsletter, The Bottom Line, formerly The Hot Sheet. Jane provides so much information about all things writing and publishing in each of her newsletters.

Next, I came across Jodi Gibson's Write Squad Community. It started with a weekly writing sprint on Instagram. Soon it morphed into a special online community, which met regularly on Zoom for writing sprints and interviews with published authors and other industry specialists. It is such a friendly group of people, mostly fairly inexperienced authors who are trying to make a go of their writing, so they are at a similar stage to me, meaning we all have similar goals and dreams. We also share the same problems, like imposter syndrome, writer's block, publishing dilemmas etc.

Another fantastic network is Pamela Cook's Writes 4 Women group, which I joined recently. She shares her experiences and the challenges of writing her novels. Pam presents a wonderful writing podcast and there are sessions every couple of weeks where we all meet on Zoom and write together. There is always something new going on. It's another great group of writerly people.

I have also been a member of Joanna Penn's Patreon group for quite a while. Joanna provides many resources, and her Patreon is totally worth the tiny monthly fee to be a part of. She does monthly Q&A sessions and live office hours sessions. She lives in the UK, so these events are mostly in the middle of the night for me. But even if I can't attend in real time, I always watch the replays and still get plenty from them.

Whilst these groups were and are fantastic, I would still like to try a face-to-face writing group as well, but that does not seem to be possible right now. I have considered starting one myself. I gave some thought to putting the word out to see if there were any writers in my area who might like to collaborate. But I guess I was concerned about just randomly trying to form a cohesive group. Most authors say that the members of a writing group need to be a good fit. What if I instigated the process and ended up with a group of people who didn't really gel? If I was responsible for setting up the group, I don't suppose I would be able to just walk away. I am still mulling over that problem. For the moment, online communities are doing the trick.

One other thing I have done is to join my first ever book club, which is a face-to-face monthly meeting and is turning out to be a wonderful opportunity to share ideas with the group and analyse a diverse range of books, some of which I might not have normally picked up.

I also have a membership with the Alliance of Independent Authors. It is quite expensive but I believe it is the best organisation for independently published authors. It is based in the United Kingdom, but as far as I am aware, there is no such organisation in Australia. Members get free access to a member forum, many useful publications and a range of other benefits, including a free annual online conference.

Now, with the guidance provided by all these fantastic resources and events, and the act of writing my books over a six-year period, I believe I am building up some knowledge and possibly even a little skill. But, like everything, so much of it comes down to practice. The learning will never end. There is always something new to learn, so the journey continues.

Key Takeaways:

- Time building networks and connections with other authors is time well spent.

- Australian authors are incredibly generous sharing their knowledge, but it can be worthwhile to invest financially in some broader networks.

- Choices need to be made as there are many worthwhile professional writer associations that provide support for authors.

Part 5: Publishing and Beyond

Boughyards Press

Self-Publishing – The Big Decision

One of the major considerations in becoming an author was how I would go about getting my books published. There are many and varied reasons to write, and although some write just for the pleasure of it, to me there seemed to be no point in writing an entire book if I couldn't get it published. At that point I had to clarify my goals. Did I want/need to make money from my books or would I be content to just have them out in the world? Was I writing just for me, for my family or for a wider audience?

I entered quite a few competitions, both for short stories and my very raw first manuscript, but I didn't have any success. Whilst I now know that my first manuscript was nowhere near ready for competition entry, I took this lack of success to indicate that I might have trouble going down the traditional publishing route. I started to explore self-publishing.

Self-published works have carried a certain stigma in the past. For a long time, they were considered inferior to traditionally published books. There was an assumption that if the manuscript had not been accepted by a traditional publisher, it simply wasn't any good. Although this perception is shifting, I think traces of it still linger.

Personally, I believe that much of the criticism of self-publishing is unwarranted. There are many self-published authors who are now presenting incredibly professional and well-written books. It was heartening to see that Michael Winkler's book, **Grimmish**, was shortlisted for the Miles Franklin Award in 2022. It was the first time a self-published novel had made it to the short list or even the long list for that matter. Michael made the tough decision to self-publish his book after many rejections. He said, 'Rightly or wrongly, being a self-published author feels undignified. Second-best.' I suspect many independent authors feel that way from time to time. I know I sometimes do. It was a boost to see it on the shortlist.

It is quite common to hear people in the industry claim that stigma has diminished, but it seems to me, there are still few mentions of self-published authors in industry news. They don't often appear on podcasts (unless the podcast is specifically about self-publishing) and mentions of self-published works in courses are also rare.

Perhaps part of the reason there may still be a certain amount of stigma, stems from the fact that some early self-published works lacked polish. With that in mind, I felt a responsibility to ensure that my books were of a high professional standard to continue to raise the profile of self-publishing as a legitimate path to publication. I am committed to making my books the best they can be.

Looking back, becoming an independently published author was not a single decision but a series of smaller ones. There were moments when I almost chose differently. At times self-publishing felt presumptuous. Who was I to put my work out into the world without the validation of a traditional publisher?

But in the end, there were a number of reasons why I finally decided to self-publish. I am not a patient person and not so young anymore. My first draft was not completed until I was 63 years old, and I knew how long it could take for publishers to even look at a manuscript. I didn't have time to wait.

The second reason is that I liked the idea of having complete control of all aspects of my book. I wanted to have a say in the cover design, the interior design and how I would sell my books. Sometimes, traditionally published authors talk about being disappointed with their covers, which I wanted to avoid. I was also able to format the book myself. And all this whilst maintaining my intellectual property.

The final factor that influenced my decision was that I love learning new things, so I wasn't afraid of all the new platforms and technologies I knew I would have to learn. But I must say it was extremely challenging. I had to learn how to get the book up to a publishable standard, how to format it, how to get the cover designed to the correct proportions, how to upload the files to the online retailers and once I had done all that, I still had to work out how to promote and market my work.

Whilst I am proud to be a self-published author, it is certainly not the pathway for the faint-hearted. Apart from the financial costs, which are covered in the Running the Business section, there are other costs as well; time, energy and emotional resilience. The mental load of learning new skills, making public mistakes and exposing my work to critique were all significant considerations.

And yet I do not regret the investment. Reward has not come from financial returns, but rather in the learning and the deep satisfaction that comes from seeing my stories in print and holding the books in my hands.

When I was considering self-publishing my work, I started looking around for available resources. I really became convinced that self-publishing could be my 'A' plan after listening to many hours of *The Creative Penn* podcast presented by Joanna Penn. She is a self-published author of over 40 books with a diverse and profitable writing business. Joanna is a firm believer in content marketing, presenting a lot of freely available information and resources in order to improve her discoverability. I have learnt so much from her. There is great content on her podcast as she interviews professionals from all areas of self-publishing, so I got to know the landscape. I also joined her mailing list and got her free book, ***Author 2.0 Blueprint***. Then I purchased her book ***Successful Self-Publishing***. This is an excellent step-by-step guide, which I followed almost to the letter. Joanna has recently published an updated version, which I have also purchased. Things change quickly, and the new version has so much additional, practical information. It also has links to many useful resources, so I will return to it regularly as I continue my author journey.

But I think the best thing I did for my self-publishing career, apart from the resources provided by Joanna Penn, was to sign up to Launchpad, previously Self-Publishing 101. This course includes hours of content on every subject imaginable about self-publishing and comes with lifetime access. The course took me through each step in the publishing process with practical video demonstrations of all the technical aspects. The only problem is that the websites and programs change so quickly that some of the "how-to" videos go out of date quickly. The developers of Launchpad do regular updates (at no additional cost) but I am sure it must be impossible to keep up with everything.

Another fabulous resource is the book called ***Look— it's your book!*** by Anna Featherstone. She has written about self-publishing from an Australian perspective. This was something I was looking for because all my other research on self-publishing had led me to people publishing in the UK or USA.

I attended a webinar with Anna through the Write with A L Tait group. As the groups that attended these sessions were small, there was plenty of opportunity to ask questions. I was able to speak to Anna directly about my process so far. I think she was a bit surprised I had set a release date that was coming up quite soon, but that I didn't appear to be sufficiently organised.

There were quite a few things I didn't have in place. One thing she recommended was distributing an Advance Information Sheet (AIS), which was new to me. An AIS is similar to a one page press release containing all the relevant information such as book descriptions, where/how to purchase and an author bio. Anna also alerted me to the library distributors. I purchased her excellent book and read up about those things and immediately put them in place. I reached out to her on social media to ask a question, and she got back to me almost immediately. I was extremely grateful that she was so willing to share her expertise. During the online session, I mentioned I had draft emails ready to send out to libraries about Author Talks and book signings, but I just hadn't been game to press send. She told me I should not say no to myself. It is okay for others to say no to you, but quite another thing to say no to yourself by not asking the question in the first place. Wise words indeed and advice that has always stuck with me.

Another consideration once I had started on the path to self-publishing was whether I wanted to produce audiobooks. Having an audiobook narrated by a professional narrator is extremely expensive. Yet, there is a growing market for audiobooks, and some readers only consume literature via audio. Added to that is the question of accessibility. Visually impaired people rely on audio. I explored the option of narrating my own books. I undertook a course called Audio Books Made Easy and purchased the recommended microphone. To date, I am yet to finish the course, and the whole audiobook project is very much still a work in progress.

Self-publishing is not for everyone. There is a lot to learn, and all the expenses related to publishing must be borne by the author and they can be substantial. But I didn't have time to wait, and I am in the fortunate position that I can afford to treat my books as a hobby. Although I do hope that my decision to self-publish eventually pays for itself.

Key Takeaways:

- Self-publishing can be the 'A' plan, but it is not for everyone.

- There is a lot to learn but there are also lots of resources available.

- Don't say no to yourself by not asking the question in the first place.

Editing and Proofing

Learning to self-edit is a journey in itself. I generally find editing an enjoyable process, even though it can be nearly as difficult as writing the first draft. Seeing the book come together from a messy beginning feels incredibly rewarding. Once again, I take inspiration from other authors. One particular process I really liked was given in an Instagram post by the amazing Jane Harper. Her books are exquisite in the way they describe the Australian landscape, from a wild Tasmanian coastline to a hot, dusty outback setting and to a thick bush scene.

She hates to cut words, so she says her approach is more like a 3D printer and less like a stone sculptor. In her post, she described her process like this. She likes to work out what's needed for the story, then build it with as little waste as possible. She doesn't like the idea of starting with a gigantic mass and whittling away excess to reveal the story. I am definitely not a sculptor, and my editing process usually involves trying to add words, including more vivid description and enhancing characterisation.

These are the steps Jane uses in her editing process as she focuses on one thing at a time.

1. Sound structure - she starts by looking at the big picture. How does the story read overall?

2. Good Writing - at this stage, she is looking for anything that will make the writing more seamless for the reader.

3. Details - then she goes back and picks up all the annoying odds and ends she glossed over at the time, for example, place and character name consistency.

4. Typos - finally she runs a grammar and spell checker. It should be noted that whilst grammar and spell checkers are useful they won't know if the wrong word is used. For example, defiantly and definitely are words that are spelt correctly but have different meanings, which will not be picked up by a spell checker.

This all seems like an excellent plan. My editing is much less structured at the moment, but I am still working on it. I would like to be able to follow these four steps rather than being all over the place like I typically am now. For example, I find it hard to overlook a typo just because I am trying to look at structure.

Much of the advice that I have read tells me it is better not to edit as you go. Just get the words down. However, I have since heard many authors say that they do, in fact, edit as they go. I can't seem to help myself. I find it difficult to remember what I have written (perhaps that says something about being an older writer) and often feel the need to re-read parts. As I am rereading, I do quite a bit of editing. I find that works for me and makes the 'real' edits easier. It probably slows the completion of my first draft somewhat, but for me, I think it is worth it. One of the reasons cited by authors who do write through without editing is that it ensures they get to the end. However, that is not a problem I share. So far, I have managed to finish all the manuscripts I have started, so I think editing as I go is the best scenario for me.

The next step for me after self-editing is always to run my manuscripts through a grammar and spell checker. I use ProWritingAid for this purpose. I am always surprised to find that although I have gone through several edits, there are still plenty of basic spelling mistakes, missing commas and a lot of passive voice in each of my manuscripts. With each book, the software enabled me to make a lot more corrections. Not that I accepted all the changes that the software suggested. I ignored a lot of the passive voice suggestions, for example, as they just didn't work. But in the end, I am always pleased with the result. I don't want to pay an editor to correct mistakes I can fix myself. That way, the editor can focus on things that software can't fix.

I always feel nervous when it is time to ask someone else to read my work. But I am not sure why because my beta readers have always been considerate and measured with their advice.

Once I get their feedback, it is time for another round of self-editing to implement their suggestions. Then, once all that has been actioned, I send it off to my professional editor for the first stages of the editing process—the structural and copy edits.

Eventually we come to the final proofread. I am fortunate to have a close friend with great attention to detail, who kindly offered to proofread all my books. It is a gigantic task, and I am extremely grateful to her. This has turned out to be a double bonus because she has told me how much she enjoyed them, which lessened my sense of imposter syndrome. Even though she is a close friend, she is also very honest, so I trust her opinion.

But even with the best editing and proofreading, there are often still minor mistakes and errors. You can find them in almost any book. Quite by accident, I came upon another great proofreading strategy. I decided I would upload my books to Google Play and create auto-narrated audiobooks.

NOTE: It is important to state here that I think that human narration is the gold standard and I would not hand that work over to a robot if I could afford to pay a human narrator. At this point, I just cannot justify the cost of having my books professionally narrated. I hope to be able to afford that one day. But it is not an option at the moment. If I didn't use AI narration for my historical fiction books, I would not have audiobooks at all.

Although I made the decision to have my audiobooks for sale on the Google Play site, I priced them cheaply and made it clear that they are not narrated by a human. I have sold only one audiobook, but that is probably because I have not promoted them at all as I am not confident that the technology is good enough yet. I know that many readers of audiobooks say that a narrator who is not to their liking can spoil a good book.

But I soon found an additional benefit. It proved to be a valuable exercise. I wanted to ensure the books sounded alright given that artificial intelligence narrated them. I listened all the way through and picked up several typos that had not been noticed in all the editing. One, in particular, in my first book was strange. I found that I frequently typed 'q' instead of 'g'. These two letters obviously look quite similar in print and would have been virtually impossible to pick up with the naked eye. But as the auto-narrator reads exactly what is written, I heard those mistakes and was able to correct them.

One benefit of self-publishing is the ability to re-upload the manuscript, even after publication, if errors are found. There were quite a few in my first book. Once they were corrected, I immediately uploaded the new manuscript.

For my subsequent manuscripts, I ensured I had listened to the auto narration before I published the books or ordered any print copies. I believe they both have far fewer errors. The only errors that have been pointed out to me in my most recent book, are a couple of date errors picked up by my readers. I was able to correct those and re-upload. No one has pointed out any errors in *Breaking Free*, which is pleasing.

Whilst the final editing was occurring, I started working on the formatting.

Key Takeaways:

- Editing as I go works for me. But everyone is different and you must find the process that works for you.

- Adding structure to the self-editing process is useful.

- Listening to auto narration is a good option for proof-reading.

Formatting and Covers

I had no idea how to format my book. I had to learn how to manage this for both ebook and print versions. This was going to be tricky. I had to decide whether to purchase some software to do it myself or pay another expert to do it for me.

I had heard a lot about Vellum. It seemed to be a popular formatting tool, but it was only available for Mac. If I wanted to use it, I would need to purchase a Mac. The other alternative I heard about was MacinCloud. By using a MacinCloud account I could apparently use Vellum on my Windows computer. But that seemed pretty complex when I looked into it. But then I heard about another, newer formatting program called Atticus. The developers of this program seemed to be focused on helping authors. I decided to try this program and found that it was completely sufficient for my needs.

Formatting was relatively simple with this tool. However, I discovered manuscripts need to have certain protocols in place prior to uploading to Atticus. I had to make sure chapter names were in Heading One format in the Word document, and scene breaks needed to have three asterisks. Once this was done, it is really just a matter of uploading the manuscript and choosing a template.

Then I had to consider front and back matter, which are an important component of book formatting. These pages contain the Title Page, Imprint or Copyright Page, Author Notes, Acknowledgments, and Also By pages. Front and back matter can be another marketing tool if done well.

The back matter included the Acknowledgements where I thanked all the people who contributed to my book. Of course, writing a book is not as solitary a pursuit as you would think. Many other people contribute along the way and need to be thanked.

I always like to include Author Notes in the back matter to provide some background about my books. I think it is important that my readers understand that, whilst my stories are based on true events, I do fictionalise them. I like to let readers know that I include my imaginings of how things might have unfolded, but at the same time, I would like them to know that my books are thoroughly researched, and that the fictionalised bits absolutely could have happened.

Interestingly, before I became a writer, I rarely read the front and back matter. I wonder if that is the case with most other readers? As I said earlier, these pages can be an important marketing tool, but is this really the case if readers don't actually read them? Now I often read these pages first before even starting a book. Perhaps that is because I realise how much I was missing by not reading them.

Once the formatting is done in Atticus, the book can be downloaded in three formats: ePub for ebooks, PDF for print and also a Microsoft Word document.

The next professional I needed to find was a cover designer. They say, 'Don't judge a book by its cover', but it seems that readers certainly do. Everything I learned suggested that the cover needs to be extremely professional and eye-catching. It needs to reflect the genre. It is another, even more important marketing tool. This time I looked at sites like Fiver and Reedsy. I tried these first but found that I was not allowing enough of a budget to entice any of the cover designers on those platforms to take on my cover. This in itself was useful because I was getting some idea of how much a professional cover would cost. I looked at other options, like creating a cover myself using software like Canva. Or I could purchase a cover that someone had already designed. But remembering all the advice about professionalism, I upped my budget and looked for a professional designer. I guess I took a bit of a risk in this case. My niece and her husband run a business called High Voltage Studio. They specialise in web design and social media content. My niece is also an emerging author and an avid reader. Her husband is an amazing graphic designer, whose work I very much admire. So I thought, why not see what they could do? That, I think, turned out to be a brilliant decision.

Conflict at Hanging Rock

The front and back matter needs to be created in Atticus in order to work efficiently. My first attempt was basic. I simply added text to the templates provided in Atticus and didn't give it much more thought.

When developing ideas for the cover of my first book, I had found a photo that I loved. It was a picture of Hanging Rock featuring a misty day, along with a dwelling in the foreground. The dwelling was a fairly modern timber house. But overall it looked exactly like what I wanted. Replace the modern dwelling with a slab hut and it would be perfect. I didn't know how a graphic designer would work with this. But I soon found out my designer would create the cover with Photoshop. So yes, it would be great if we could use that photo. I contacted the website that featured the image to see what the usage rights were for the photo. Unfortunately, we could not use that photo. Then, we searched for photos available for purchase. The designer got back to me within days with a rough mock-up of the front cover. I was delighted with the basics of it immediately. He had found a fantastic photo of Hanging Rock, which was perfect. However, the slab hut was not as I imagined. I gave him feedback to that effect and waited to see what he came up with next. He then came back to me to say that whilst he had found a good hut photo that was reasonably priced, the photo of Hanging Rock was way too expensive to purchase. He decided he would go to Hanging Rock and take a photo for the cover himself and got a brilliant shot. I think the cover looks amazing.

Ebooks only require the front cover but for print books, the wraparound cover needs to be designed, including the back of the book blurb and placement of the ISBN and barcode which my print books need to have in order to be published. The IBSN is the International Book Standard Number assigned to each specific edition and format of a book. I had to purchase these from Thorpe Bowker, the official agency for ISBNs in Australia. Each format, print, ebook, audio, and large print all need to have a separate ISBN. It is not mandatory to have an ISBN for ebooks, but I decided to allocate one to all formats.

I also had to work out what the spine dimensions would be. Fortunately, there are online spine size calculators, which are fairly simple to use once you know the exact number of pages that will be in the book.

As an author I never get over the feeling of holding my book for the first time. Holding it up and saying, 'I made this' is a totally uplifting feeling. But I had mixed feelings when I first laid eyes on this precious first book. My proof from Amazon arrived much sooner than I expected, so I was excited to rip open the package. Proofs from Amazon have a band around the cover saying not for resale, which of course spoils the look a little. Those from the other print on demand distributor, Ingram Spark, don't have this little spoiler on the cover.

My book was only 55,600 words, and even though I knew it would be small, I was unprepared for my emotions upon seeing it. I hadn't seen a book of that size in years. All modern fiction books are 300 or more pages. My 200-page book looked tiny.

Because it seemed so small, I then began to doubt whether I had priced it correctly. I had compared the prices of other books in the genre, and I did price it lower, but was it low enough? I would have to make a decision and then go back and make the price changes if that was what I decided.

And then I noticed the tiny white space at the bottom of the cover. I hadn't gotten the dimensions right. I would have to get back to my designer to make some tweaks.

I was somewhere between elated and devastated. It was an emotional roller coaster. How could I be experiencing both of these feelings at the same time?

The silly thing about all this was that I knew that the book was going to be small, and I knew the cover might need some tweaks. It is hard to understand why I felt so down. I think it had all just been so overwhelming and so hard to get to this stage. Surely, it must get easier at some point.

The proofs from IngramSpark were supposed to arrive on the same day, but they were delayed. Another disappointment. But when they did arrive, I started feeling slightly better. The covers were perfect, as was the internal content, so I was able to order three cartons so that I had some to sell.

I eventually got over my disappointment at the first sight of my book and looked forward to selling some. I decided not to change the prices and just see how sales went.

Breaking Free

By now I had learnt more about the marketing advantages of front and back matter pages, so with my second book I made some changes. For one thing, I included requests for reviews and a newsletter signup link. Although I haven't had a lot of newsletter subscribers coming from these pages, many authors find they do get results this way.

For the cover of my second book, I wanted an old image I had found of the Kew Lunatic Asylum to feature in the background. The only other stipulation I had for the brief was to add a woman with a large hat. My great-grandmother wore an amazing hat on her wedding day. The decorations adorning the hat would have to be around 20 centimetres tall. At first, I thought the image that the designer suggested looked a bit too modern. But we went ahead anyway. When I saw the finished cover, I loved it. I was absolutely delighted. I felt quite emotional.

Then when it came time to create the wraparound cover I discovered the two print on demand services I was using had template creation tools, which took a lot of the pain out of this process.

The sense of euphoria was certainly there when the print copy of my second book arrived. It was perfect and required no tweaks. The cover of *Breaking Free* is still my favourite, so when I held the proof copy in my hand I was elated. The formatting was great, and having listened to the auto narration prior to publication, I was confident there were no typos in it.

Family & Fortune

By the time I came to format my third book, I noticed some authors had About the Author and Also By pages at the beginning of the book. I learnt that if I put those pages at the front, they will show up in the online retailers' previews. This provides another way that readers might go to my website and see what else I have written. This time, I also added a link to my email subscription and review request on my About the Author page, so that is front and centre as well.

The other page I included at the back of *Family & Fortune* is another Also By page with images and descriptions of my other books. After some tweaking this worked well and I intend to revise all of my books to include this additional Also By page when time permits.

The cover for this book took a bit more back and forwarding with my designer. Once again, I wanted a woman on the cover with the Castlemaine goldfields in the background. We found some images of women that would have been perfect, but they were incredibly expensive and the copyright on them only lasted a couple of years. I did not want to have to change the cover that quickly, especially if I was paying such an exorbitant sum. Eventually we found a suitable image. We had a couple of choices for the background image. I decided to ask my newsletter subscribers. I put a poll in my newsletter, and whilst there were votes for both versions, 60% of those who voted chose the cover I finally decided on. It turns out that I love the finished cover.

One issue that seems to occur no matter how carefully the cover template is designed, is that the spine can sometimes bleed onto the front and back covers. We took that out of the equation with *Family & Fortune* by making the background image of the front cover wrap right around. However, this presented another problem, which I didn't notice until the book was published and printed. Because the background of the front image was rather pale, the spine does not stand out well in a book stack or on the shelf if it is not facing out and only the spine is showing. You learn something (or really multiple things) with every new book. It is not a huge issue as, being self-published, the book is not likely to appear in a lot of bookshops. But that is another story.

My third book is a good, chunky book with over 300 pages. It also has a great cover that I am extremely pleased with. I was definitely delighted when the proofs arrived. Once again, I had listened to the auto-narration to catch any last-minute typos.

Now that all three books are published you might think that everything is finalised. However, I do want to make some tweaks to the book description on the retails sites and update the front and back matter so that all the books are similar. For me, as a self-published author, that is simply a matter of updating the files in Atticus, logging on to my accounts on the retail sites and re-uploading the books or changing descriptions or meta data.

High Voltage Studio has designed all my covers, and I love them all. It is such a buzz to reveal the cover each time. I usually do a post on social media revealing a section and then do the full reveal a few days later. All the covers have received great feedback.

I suppose, although writing and producing a book does not get easier, it has for me become more rewarding as I learn more and publish each new book.

But once I had the proofs in my hands and I was completely happy with everything about them, there was still the tricky process of publishing and distributing the books.

Key Takeaways:

- Formatting is straightforward but it pays to create front and back matter that can also act as a marketing tool.

- Book covers are so important because readers really do judge books by their cover.

- Ordering a proof copy of the book is an essential step to ensure everything is correct before ordering bulk copies.

- Take advantage of the full book cover templates offered by the printing companies.

Publishing and Distribution

Distribution is another vital part of the process. The first decision I had to make was where to publish and whether I would be exclusive with Amazon or publish widely. If I went exclusively with Amazon, I could not publish my books on other platforms, so it seemed a simple choice not to do this.

Another important reason that I didn't want to go exclusive was that I think many people in Australia buy their books through Booktopia. Unfortunately Booktopia has been through some difficulties in recent times. Hopefully, it is back on track for good now.

Ingram Spark and Draft2Digital are what is known as aggregator publishers. Once a book is uploaded to their websites, it is distributed to a wide range of online stores and the books are available to be purchased by brick and mortar book stores and also libraries.

For print books, the best options seem to be Amazon (non-exclusive) and IngramSpark. They both offer Print on

Demand, which meant I wouldn't need to order a full print run of, say, 500 or more books. A book only gets printed when I, the author, order it, or when a customer orders it from an online retailer or bookshop.

Ingram Spark distributes to all the retailers, including Booktopia, Dymocks and Barnes & Noble. Once I upload my books to Ingram Spark, they appear in the online stores of all these retailers and more as well. By publishing to both Amazon and Ingram Spark, my books are widely distributed.

For the ebooks, Draft2Digital appeared to be the best option. They also publish widely to a large range of ebook retailers. My books are available on sites such as Kindle, Kobo, Nook and Apple Books, to name a few. Draft2Digital also has an author page, which can be useful. Another benefit of Draft2Digital is that they provide a Universal Book Link (UBL). This single link points to all the retailers where the book is available. When I share this link on my social media or my website, it allows customers to purchase the book from the store of their choice. If there are links that are not picked up by the UBL, I can amend or add my own links. However, this UBL doesn't currently allow me to add the link to my website shop. There are other places I can get a UBL. BookFunnel is one such place, and it now allows authors to include links to their own websites so I will be investigating that.

All my books are also available to libraries and bookstores through Ingram Spark for print and Draft2Digital for ebooks.

Unfortunately, having physical books in bookstores is unusual for self-published authors. Without the backing of a publishing house, it is quite difficult to get books into bookstores without a lot of work of physically visiting individual stores and requesting they stock your book. But my books are available if someone requests them from a bookstore or a library. I talked to my local bookstore owner, and she agreed to stock my books. I am exceedingly grateful for her support.

Before publishing, I had done a lot of homework about what I would need to have in place in order to upload my books to all these retailers. The two excellent books I have previously mentioned helped me with this process. *Successful Self-publishing* by Joanna Penn gave me a step-by-step approach, and *Look– it's your book!* by Anna Featherstone gave me some great general tips.

The publishing process was reasonably straightforward because, after all the research I had done, I knew what to do and what information I would need to provide. I created a document for each book containing all the relevant information, known as metadata. These documents included the book description, my author bio, the ISBNs for each format and all the other sundry information so I had it at my fingertips ready to key in. Other important parts of this metadata are the categories and keywords. Categories are where the book will show up on the retailer listings. For example, my books come under categories such as historical fiction and Australian fiction. Keywords help the algorithms to recommend books to readers.

Finding the best categories and keywords can be tricky, which is why I invested in a program called Publisher Rocket to help with this task. Having all this metadata ready ended up saving quite a chunk of time and eased the anxiety a bit because I felt organised as I went through the process. I felt like I knew what I was doing, at least to some extent. I did feel quite stressed when it came to completing the US tax form so that I wouldn't be charged the full taxation amount for sales in the US. That was a bit confusing, but it seems I worked it out as I am only being charged 5% tax for any sales in the US instead of the 30% I would be charged if I hadn't completed the form.

Early on, I found one of the few things I could not control as a self-published author. It had not occurred to me, and neither had I read it anywhere in my research, that retailers would set their own price. I just assumed that they would use the recommended retail price I had set with the distributors. And most retailers did. But I was horrified when I checked on Booktopia and the price being charged for *Conflict at Hanging Rock* was $15 more than the Recommended Retail Price that I had set. When it was on pre-order, they had only added a couple of dollars. I couldn't understand why they would add so much. The main reason for my annoyance was I felt if customers paid that amount for it, they would be disappointed. Not because it is not a good book, but because it is only 55,000 words, a much smaller book than many others of the same genre. Fortunately, after some time, the price reverted to what it had been when first published on the site. But I have often asked myself whether that cost me sales in that critical first week.

Conflict at Hanging Rock

When I was ready to publish my first book, I worked on getting the book uploaded to Ingram Spark first. I set up my account, which was relatively easy. I set the publication date and went ahead with the upload. As I did all this before the publication date I had set, the book was available for pre-order. Finally, it was done, and now I had to wait. I was concerned about the print book cover because I had ended up with about 8 pages less than I had when I calculated the spine width. This was because of the formatting, which had left spare pages after some chapters. I contacted the help desk at Atticus, and they promptly told me how to solve this problem. Fortunately, 8 pages did not affect the spine.

When I uploaded *Conflict at Hanging Rock*, I made the mistake of publishing both the ebook and the paperback with Ingram Spark because I saw the cost was the same whether I uploaded just the print book or both. However, it wasn't long before I realized this was not the best process. However, I later discovered that Draft2Digital is the platform recommended by most indie authors for ebooks. I uploaded my ebook there as well. It was quick and easy.

Then I was worried about the ebook still being available on Ingram Spark. Further investigation told me I needed to email them to ask them to unlist it. They responded quickly, and the ebook soon appeared on the Ingram Spark dashboard as cancelled. They said that it might take up to 180 days to clear it completely, but I didn't think that would be a concern. Especially as it was only on pre-order at that point. But I am glad I took that action.

Once I had Ingram Spark and Draft2Digital displaying the pre-order of my book, I turned to Amazon. The first step was to set up my account on Kindle Direct Publishing (KDP) so I could publish on that platform. Then, I was able to create a print version of my book, once again using the metadata I had previously gathered. I saved it in draft form because I needed to get a proof copy before it went live. I didn't create the ebook on Amazon at the same time because I couldn't see how to create it without letting it go live.

I think one of the biggest challenges I faced was the timing of all these components. I wanted to do some early promotion, but I had no idea how to do that when I hadn't yet published and therefore didn't know for sure where the books would be available.

Setting a publication date seemed necessary, and yet I didn't know when I would have physical books in my hands. I didn't know when to upload the books to the different distributors to make sure they would be available by the date I'd set.

Breaking Free

I learned so much in the writing and publishing of that first book, which did make the second somewhat easier. Although, having a gap of more than a year between the publishing of these two books, I forgot a lot of what I had learnt. Things change over time too, which also needs to be taken into account. One thing that had changed was that there was no longer a fee to upload to Ingram Spark, which was one less cost.

When I had published *Breaking Free*, I discovered that it would be a good idea to upload my books to Kobo directly as opposed to making them available on that platform through Draft2Digital. There are several benefits. Firstly they have a subscription model called Kobo Plus. This is similar to Amazon's Kindle Unlimited, which allows people to obtain books via a monthly subscription. Unlike Amazon's Kindle Unlimited, you don't have to be exclusive with Kobo to access this model. I could still have my ebooks distributed to all the other platforms through Draft2Digital. Another benefit is that Kobo has some great promotions available at reasonable prices; some are even free. Unfortunately, lots of authors apply for these promotions, so it is quite difficult to get a place. However, I have managed to get into a couple. One in particular that was quite successful was the Kobo Plus list feature. In Kobo Plus, payment is made according to reading minutes. I had excellent results from this promotion, and my books are definitely being read through that platform. But as my books were already being distributed to Kobo through Draft2Digital I had to wait for them to unlist the books before Kobo would accept them. But it was well worth the effort.

Family & Fortune

For my most recent novel, *Family & Fortune*, I have kept what I hope are more thorough notes about the processes, hoping that next time there won't be too many changes and I will have something to refer back to. One new thing I discovered was that there can be problems between KDP and Ingram Spark when using the same ISBN. Of course, I knew I had to use the same ISBN, so I wasn't sure why there would be a problem. I hadn't encountered any issues previously, but I was keen to avoid any now. I discovered it was best to upload the book to KDP without a future date and save it as a draft rather than publishing it with a future date. Once the Amazon approval process was completed, the book could be uploaded to Ingram Spark with no chance of any issues occurring.

As well as selling through the online retailers, I wanted to sell direct. Cutting out the middleman would, of course, provide a larger percentage of each sale directly to my bank account. By selling direct, I could also offer signed copies.

This presented me with a lot more to learn and another raft of decisions to make. I researched Shopify, which is a direct sales ecommerce site that is used by many authors. It can be a complete website, or I could use it as a sales platform and continue to maintain my existing Squarespace website. The major benefit of Shopify is that it has an integration with Print on Demand (POD), so you don't have to worry about mailing out the print books. Shopify sends the order automatically to the POD company, and the book is printed and sent directly to the customer. However, after giving it plenty of thought, I decided I wasn't ready to create a whole new website, which would incur an additional cost. I decided to stick with selling on my existing website. And after all, at that stage I wasn't expecting to have to post a lot of books, which is how things have eventuated. I still don't sell many books through my website. I will certainly keep my options open and may decide on a different platform as my business expands.

To have ecommerce meant I had to have a higher Squarespace plan, but it would still work out cheaper than going with Shopify. I upgraded to the Business Plan, which costs approximately an extra $100 per annum. It does not have all the benefits of the full ecommerce plan, but the major difference that it would make for my needs was that with the Business Plan there is a 3% transaction fee, which would not apply if I chose the higher plans. However, I did not envisage high sales through my website, so I felt it was worth not paying for the higher plan.

It was a little tricky trying to work out the ecommerce functionality on Squarespace. It was easy enough for the print book. But the ebook was a different story. Sure, there was a function to upload an ebook for sale. However, then I would probably be faced with queries about how to download the book. This apparently has been a perennial problem, so much so that it has its own terminology. It is called sideloading. However, with BookFunnel, a service which I had already been using to distribute my free ebook, I knew that would not be a problem as they provide support for readers to download the ebook. So to facilitate the sale of ebooks, I use the function, which allows for the sale of a service on my website. When the order comes through, an automated email is sent to the purchaser to confirm the purchase and inform them that further information about the download will be forthcoming. Then I send an email with the link to the ebook on BookFunnel. Although delivery of the ebook would be delayed until I saw the order come through, it seemed to be a suitable solution. I am not completely satisfied with my online shop despite all the work I have done to try to improve it. I hope to be able to afford to get a web developer to have a look at it eventually. But that would be another cost that I am not ready to pay out yet.

Shipping was another consideration. Once I had decided to do the packing and shipping of print books myself, I had to add shipping costs. The cost of postage is substantial. To begin with, I just added a standard cost with no variations. Later I added an international charge, but I have not yet sold any print books directly from my website outside of Australia, so there has been no opportunity to test out that system. I eventually discovered that I could also add a hand-delivered option by adding my home postcode. I could then offer free delivery to anyone whom I could hand deliver to.

Selling direct from my website also meant that I needed to consider international taxes. Most countries have a threshold that needs to be reached before any taxes are charged. It seems unlikely that I would ever reach that sort of revenue from selling direct. So far, I have only sold to Australian customers on my website. But I went ahead and tried to organise a reporting mechanism for the EU and UK. I did this through an organisation called The VAT EAS compliance platform. They were helpful, but whilst I now have a system for the EU, I was unable to arrange anything for the UK. I was told later that I didn't need to register unless I was likely to reach the threshold, but I have not been able to conclusively confirm that. It is a moot point anyway because I have had no sales in the UK or EU to date.

I also wanted to sell direct at events. Many people do not carry cash these days so I thought it would be important to have a Point Of Sale facility. After doing some research, I decided Square would be the best option because I could create a free account and then purchase a portable card reader for a reasonable price. More recently, there is a facility to use Square on an iPhone app, which is straightforward and saves having to have the card reader on hand. I have sold a lot of books through author talks at libraries and I also had a stall at the Clunes Book Fair in 2024 and although it was a tiring weekend I sold quite a few books and met lots of readers.

Another pathway to get books into readers' hands is through libraries. Not everyone can afford to buy books, so if I wanted everyone to have access to my books and become more widely recognised, being in libraries was important. At first, I thought that having the book distributed through Ingram Spark would be sufficient for libraries to search for and purchase it, but apparently not. It seemed I needed to get my book listed in library catalogues run by a range of library distributors.

When I had finished *Conflict at Hanging Rock*, I checked out ALS Library Services and completed their online form. Soon I had an email response from them saying they needed me to send them a physical copy of the book. Once I had sent the first book and had it approved, all subsequent books have been accepted without my having to provide print copies.

I also contacted James Bennett Library Distributors and downloaded the new book information form that was provided on their website. I completed that and sent it off via email along with my book cover.

After about six weeks, my first order came through from ALS Library Services. It was only for two books, but I was excited. That meant that my books were being requested at another library. However, since then, I have not had any orders through these library distributors. Yet I know that several libraries have my books. Perhaps these additional distributors are not so critical.

Apart from accessibility, another benefit of having books in libraries is the Public Lending Rights (PLR) scheme. This government scheme compensates authors for loss of sales from free lending. But in order to receive a payment, there must be at least 50 copies of each book in libraries around Australia. As far as I am aware, I am still a long way away from that total for any of my books, but I have registered all my books with the scheme, so maybe one day.

Once my books are published and have been distributed, promotion is the next step.

Key Takeaways:

- The best option for print books is to distribute through Ingram Spark and Amazon Print on Demand services.

- Draft2Digital and Kobo are best for ebooks.

- Books can be purchased by Libraries through Ingram Spark and Draft2Digital. But it is a good idea to also register with the Australian Library Service and James Bennett Library Distributors.

- Selling direct through Squarespace is complex but worth it for the better financial return.

- Selling direct at events has proven successful.

Marketing and Promotion

Marketing and promotion are vital parts of the work of a self-published author. If I was to get some returns for all the hard work I had put into writing my books, I knew I would need to learn a lot more about this important process.

Marketing is about building customer relationships, creating brand awareness and providing a great customer experience, including after-sales service. This part is not so daunting and is a continual process over many years.

Promotion, on the other hand, is the bit where I have to make my book available and discoverable. I need to tell people about my books and ask them whether they would like to purchase them. This is the difficult bit for an introvert like me.

Discoverability is problematic when there are so many out-standing books on the market and new ones are being published every day. Bringing my books to the attention of readers who would enjoy them was always going to be difficult. Even my family and friends would not buy my books if they didn't know where or how to purchase them. Complete strangers would have no chance. I had to decide what would be the best strategy to launch the books, how to let people know they were available and where to purchase them.

Some self-published authors rely on services offered by hybrid publishing organisations to help with marketing and promotion. Traditionally published authors have a marketing team to help with this. Although, even traditionally published authors are being required to do more of their own marketing and promotion these days. I decided to take on these tasks myself. The entire process is completely up to me.

Do I enjoy marketing? Well, compared to long walks by the lake where I live, I would say, definitely not. It ranks somewhere near cleaning the shower. What I do enjoy is reaching new readers and interacting online with people who might take the time to read my book. In any case, I had to get over myself and get on with it. This is definitely not my favourite part of the process.

Conflict at Hanging Rock

Once the first book was ready, I needed to think about how to launch it. I had to set a publication date when I would make the book available on all the retail sites. Once the proofs were in my hand, I finally had the confidence to set the date. I didn't know what would be a suitable or preferable date, but I eventually randomly decided on 13th July 2022. Although unlucky for some, thirteen is my lucky number, so why not?

Having set the date, I started planning the things I still had to put in place to get the promotion under way.

Social media is one avenue. I have always been on social media but only for following family and friends' news and the occasional post. The need to increase my presence was not something I looked forward to, but I knew I had to give it a go.

It was hard to know how much reach I was getting and how often I would need to post. Many people recommend posting frequently, even several times a day. But I wondered about that, because as I amassed a small following, I noticed that the same people seemed to be interacting with my posts. Did this mean that they were the only ones my posts were being served to? This made me think twice. Surely my followers would get sick of seeing my posts. When I published my first book, I had quite a few followers on Twitter. Twitter is ephemeral. Posts get swallowed up in the feed quickly. I felt confident in posting frequently on that platform. But on the other hand, despite having more followers on Twitter than any other social media platform at that time, I didn't get a lot of engagement. As we all know, Twitter, or X as it is now called, has changed substantially in recent times, so I rarely even visit that platform these days. As time went on, I tried to leverage social media a bit more. I had good traffic on Facebook for a couple of posts, but others were quite poor. I was also building a following on Instagram, and I thought my presence there was improving, although there was still work to do.

I sought advice about whether to create an Author Page on Facebook in addition to my personal profile. The advice was that I probably didn't have time to get enough followers before the publication of my first book. However, I discovered I needed a page in order to use Facebook Ads. I went ahead. I had used Facebook ads in my previous occupation, so at the time I was quite confident. I was just not sure about whether to use them to grow my mailing list prior to publishing any books or whether I should wait until the book was published and use ads for sales.

Social media is only one small part of an author's online presence. The conventional wisdom points to the need to have an author platform long before a book is published.

I suppose the point is that whilst social media platforms can be useful to build connections, the algorithms that control what is served to users can and do change at any time. Or the platform could lose favour or simply disappear.

As an author, I needed to have my own piece of real estate on the Internet. A website is crucial. A place that I own and that is not dependent on someone else's platform. I took the plunge and set up my website with Squarespace in July 2021, well before the launch of *Conflict at Hanging Rock* a year later.

I decided to use Squarespace because I had used it before in a work setting. I felt I had a bit of a head start with its functionality. It is a bit expensive, particularly when considering e-commerce. Perhaps I should have looked more closely at alternatives. But for now, I continue to use Squarespace. My website was quite basic to begin with. It had an About page, a blog and a newsletter signup.

I also needed a professional photo, so I arranged a session with a photographer. The photo was great, but I would have liked a few different versions. Looking at other authors' websites, I see that they often have a range of photos. Anyway, at least I had one good photo, which was now on my website.

When *Conflict at Hanging Rock* finally launched on that fateful Wednesday, I had mixed results. There were some immediate sales, and within a week I had probably sold around 100 copies, both print and ebook, including books I sold directly to family and friends. People were sharing my post about the launch, and it seemed as if things might go well. I even got a couple of fantastic reviews, and one of those was from a person from the UK whom I hadn't even previously connected with. But after about a week, sales just stopped. Not just slowed down, completely stopped. Obviously, I needed to ramp things up.

Fortunately, I had library talks coming up quite soon, so I hoped the publicity for those would get things moving again.

Library talks are a good marketing and promotional tool. The libraries advertised my talks on their websites and on their socials, and I also shared the dates on my social media and my website events page. The attendance was reasonable. There were around 20 people at each event. I have heard some authors say that they have given talks where only one or two people turned up, so I was happy with my attendances. But despite the time I had put into planning, the early days of promotion were haphazard.

I needed a way to reach people outside my small networks and build relationships with my existing and new readers. Content marketing can be an effective way to reach readers. I wanted to create content that might engage people who would be interested in reading my books.

Starting a newsletter became the best solution—it gives me direct access to subscribers who have explicitly chosen to hear from me and are genuinely interested in my books. Through it, I can connect personally with readers who want to be part of my writing journey.

As part of my newsletter strategy, I had to develop my series of onboarding emails to welcome new subscribers. These are set up as automations so that whenever someone signs up, they automatically get these two emails over a period of a week.

I also needed to decide on a giveaway, which is known as a lead magnet, to entice people to sign up. I had nothing that I could use to begin with. But once my first manuscript was almost ready for publishing, I released the first chapter as my giveaway.

As the book was partially set in Melbourne, I also added some information about the new city in the 1860s.

I realised my mailing list was going to be really important, so I worked hard to encourage new subscribers. My first strategy to get subscribers was to post on social media when my newsletter was due to come out, asking people to sign up. This resulted in one or two subscribers each month, which was better than nothing. I then decided to try a Facebook ad. Asking people to sign up for my newsletter when I had little to offer was difficult, and to do it with an ad that many people were going to see made it even more daunting. I was not even sure it would be terribly useful. The ad ran for 3 days, and I only had three people sign up. Still, I suppose that is three people I wouldn't have had otherwise. I actually felt quite pleased when I saw their sign-ups. Small steps all add up in the long run. At the end of the ad campaign, my subscribers numbered 28. Apart from gathering subscribers, I thought this was a useful way to try out the process of paid advertising on Facebook, even though there would be no direct financial return. When I published my first book, I had 34 subscribers, which was starting to build.

Deciding on the best platform for newsletters has been difficult. When I started, I used Mailchimp. My reasoning for using that platform was that I had used it before, so I had a bit of an idea of how it functioned.

Breaking Free

As I was getting ready to publish my second book, I once again had to focus on promotion. Knowing everything I now did about the importance of having an email list, I tried another Facebook Ad offering a free ebook copy of *Conflict at Hanging Rock*. I signed up for a free course delivered by Learn Self-Publishing, which stepped me through how to do a Facebook ad to obtain leads. This turned out to be quite successful. I ran the ad for 7 days, and for the cost of $70, I had nearly 100 new subscribers to add to my email newsletter. Many of these are still subscribers who regularly open my monthly emails.

Once I had published *Breaking Free*, I tried some Written Word Media (WWM) promotions. WWM is a platform that offers many types of promotions across a wide range of genres. The first campaign was a subscriber promotion where people who signed up for my newsletter could download a free digital copy of my new book. This promotion was successful, adding nearly 200 subscribers. But I made a big error here. Lists of email subscribers had to be downloaded from the WWM website. I downloaded the first list without realising there would be a second group to download, which I found many months later. I added them to my subscribers list despite the delay and sent them my welcome email explaining what had happened and hoped that they would still be interested in my newsletter. Many of them opened my newsletters, which was a relief.

By now I was building quite a good email list, but I wasn't completely happy with the Mailchimp platform. I tried MailerLite, and it was great. Many more features are available for free. However, another problem soon arose. Not long after I had signed up with my Gmail address, I discovered that I could have an email linked to my domain name through an agreement between GoDaddy, where my paulinewilson.com.au domain is hosted, and Office 365. So I had the new address. That was an exciting advance for me, but it meant that I now needed to change the address my newsletters were coming from. To do that, I needed to add a new user, which wasn't an option with the free plan as it only allowed for one user. I had to change to a paid plan, even though the additional features on offer with the increased plan were not required.

I started to get some comments and emails from my newsletter subscribers, which I was thrilled to receive. That people would take the time not only to read my newsletters but to write a response was extremely heartening. I am always careful to respond to everyone who takes the time to contact me. I want it to be a two-way conversation as much as possible. Some readers might wonder whether we authors really do like hearing from our readers. But I would like to assure readers that all the authors I know love to hear from them. I certainly am one such author, so I urge readers not to think that they are being a nuisance by contacting me. I love to hear from you.

I tried another one of WWM's Bargain Booksy promotions in late 2023 when *Breaking Free* was first released. It didn't produce a lot of sales, but it was good to try it out.

One thing that is often touted as a great marketing idea is to write more books. When I did my first author talks in the Riverina district of New South Wales in 2024, I had published two books, so had plenty to talk about, and some attendees at my talks bought copies of both books. I could definitely see the benefit of continuing to write and publish more books as another marketing tool.

Just before *Breaking Free* was published, I decided my website needed more work. I signed up for a course at the Australian Writers Centre for website design. I couldn't justify the cost of employing a professional to improve my website, so this was the next best thing. The first part of the course was about establishing a brand, including fonts and colours. The course recommended creating a Pinterest board to gather some ideas. This part took an inordinate amount of time as I tried to decide on fonts and colours to match my brand. The major complication was all the platforms didn't seem to have the same fonts. I needed to match the fonts on all the various parts of my author platform. I eventually settled for some similar fonts where I couldn't match them exactly. Then there were colours. Some authors match their brand colours to their books, which looks great but means a website/brand update for each new book. I had used a lot of blue as it matched my first book cover, so I continued with blue but also added a sand colour and a shade of yellow. At the same time, I developed a style guide, which has been helpful.

My website was becoming quite extensive. It had home and about pages and a page for each of my books, for events, my shop, my blog and a contact page. I still had only one professional author photo, so I added a few less professional but passable versions.

In December 2023, I decided I would prefer to have every-thing in one place, so I moved my subscribers to Squarespace and started using that for my monthly emails. I was not sure it was the best decision as I soon discovered it does not have the same level of functionality as the sites specifically designed for email distribution, and there is an additional cost for email campaigns.

Family & Fortune

One new strategy I tried for the release of my third book was to get some reviews through Booksprout. This is a website where an author can offer the book for free and readers sign up to read it and commit to providing a review. Unfortunately, I had only about five people download the book and only a couple of them actually left reviews. So that was not terribly successful.

In May 2025, I took part in another WWM subscriber campaign, this time offering *Family & Fortune* in return for a newsletter signup. I got well over 300 new subscribers.

I still wasn't completely happy with my website, so in November 2024, as I was finishing *Family & Fortune*, I did some more updates, changing the colours yet again.

I was now writing regular monthly newsletters, trying to be consistent, sending them on the first Wednesday of each month at the same time. It can be rather difficult coming up with interesting content for newsletters, which is one reason I decided on only writing monthly. But as I have learnt more by reading lots of other authors' newsletters, I have refined my offering and now my newsletter subscribers know to expect some of the same things that I write each month. I review the books I have read, talk a bit about my work in progress, and I add a fun fact. Recently, I have occasionally added a short story.

I am now trying to widen the net by publishing another monthly newsletter on Substack on the alternate fortnight. This platform is a whole new learning curve, but many authors have good things to say about it. It seems easier to get new subscribers, rather than just through links in the back matter of my books and my website signup form. However, I wonder if it will develop into something similar to social media. I guess there is also the chance that it could be sold to a Zuckerberg or a Musk. For the moment it seems useful but given my doubts about the future of Substack, I am keeping my main newsletter where it is.

When I published my first book, I had 34 subscribers, and now as I write this, I have around 500 subscribers, which I am quite satisfied with. I usually have an open rate of over 40%, which I am told is quite reasonable. Each month I see people opening who haven't done so before, so that is pleasing. I have only 3 or 4 unsubscribes every month, which is also not too bad. I thought there would be a lot more among those who signed up during the promotions to get the free book. But that has not really eventuated, although there is still a significant number who have never opened my newsletter. I could 'clean' them from my list, but as I get new opens each month and I don't need to worry about extra costs associated with large subscriber numbers yet, I am leaving them for the moment.

I still don't get a lot of organic subscribers from my website sign up page, which is something I want to work on. I am not sure why people do not sign up, especially considering my lead magnet is a complete ebook copy of *Conflict at Hanging Rock*. But I am developing good relationships with quite a few of my subscribers, and there are a couple of fans who buy all my books, for which I am forever grateful.

Some may think it strange to be giving away such a lot of free books. But as an emerging author, I think it is worth it to let more readers know about my books. Plenty of people sign up for these deals and don't get to read the book for years, if at all. But even if half of them read the books, I am happy, and there may be one or two who become fans and perhaps even purchase my other books.

Most recently, I also signed up for a BookFunnel promotion. BookFunnel is a platform primarily for direct sales of ebooks, but with other services as well, including promotions. They are free and organised by BookFunnel users. I don't think that it led to many sales, if any. But I do have the option of organising my own promotion, maybe contacting some similar authors to collaborate with on a promotion. It's something I might try in the future.

I have doubts about whether this type of promotion works well for little-known authors. And there seems to be a lot of focus on the USA and UK, so I am still assessing whether they really work for Australian authors. They may work well for authors who are better known than I.

But now with three books, I feel more confident in venturing into a full paid advertising campaign. I am still trying to learn the ins and outs of paid advertising on both Facebook and Amazon. With the introduction of AI into the process of creating ads, everything is constantly changing, so in order not to throw away my limited advertising budget, I need to continue learning to ensure that I know what I am doing before I go ahead.

I received a credit from Amazon for $100 worth of advertising, but it had to be done on Amazon.com as opposed to on Amazon.com.au, the Australian version of the website, where I expected to get significantly more sales. But I took up the offer hoping to try out the process and used most of the credit. I finished up with not a lot more knowledge and despite having the credit, Amazon still debited my account for some advertising fees, which I still don't understand.

I continue to have a love-hate relationship with social media, and I am certainly not as active as I need to be to make an impact on these platforms. It is just not something I enjoy. I would be happy never to have to post anything, but I know it is one way to develop a relationship with readers and other authors. The most beneficial part of social media for me so far has been the contact and networking with other authors. These relationships are incredibly valuable, especially as writing is often a solitary pursuit. Other authors provide support and help me keep on track when things are not going well, which is often the case.

My main social media platforms now are Facebook and Instagram. My preferred platform is definitely Instagram, but I think many of my ideal readers prefer Facebook. I am slowly building my followers on both platforms and getting good engagement with some of my posts. Despite advice to the contrary, I don't do many videos and even fewer posts where I put my face in them. I know I need to do these types of posts where I actually show myself but find it really daunting. I also find it hard to continually come up with interesting things to post. Although when I have something to say, I am happy to post. But I am determined to keep working on it. The need to keep momentum on Instagram is clear because I only get new followers when I post regularly, and the number of followers actually drops quickly when I don't post for some time. I also have accounts on Bluesky, Mastedon and Threads, but apart from sharing my Instagram posts to Threads, I barely use these platforms. Many authors are having success with BookTok in TikTok, and it is increasing sales for them. I have a TikTok account but have only posted once. As I have already noted, videos are not my thing, so TikTok is not for me.

Another issue with social media is that the platforms always seem to be changing, and I can never be entirely sure what reach I am getting. Some authors have left Facebook and Instagram, but for the moment I intend to keep learning and experimenting.

Reviews are another important promotional tool. But getting them is definitely not as easy as just asking for them or hoping they will appear. There is the option of sending out Advance Reader Copies (ARCs), which is something I have done, and have received some fantastic reviews from early readers. But finding the right people to send ARC's to can be difficult. I do occasionally ask my newsletter readers to please post a review if they have read and enjoyed any of my books . Not everyone wants to post reviews online but will send me a review via email. I have a section on my website where I post these reviews. I also have requests for reviews in the back matter of all my books. So far, I only have a handful of online reviews for each book. I am not at all sure how to get more. Perhaps the only way is to have more people read my books. So that could be another valid reason for giving them away. The more books out there, the more likelihood of reviews.

The other factor is that, apparently, Amazon advertising is not terribly successful for books that don't have many reviews. I am not sure whether I need to wait longer before I try that form of promotion. Most of my reviews have been on Goodreads, which is owned by Amazon, so perhaps those reviews might count when doing Amazon advertising. Another thing that I really need to investigate.

The other side of the coin with reviews is that some of them will invariably be bad. I know that not everyone will like my books, so I know to expect critical reviews.

Lots of authors don't read their reviews, but I think I have a thick enough skin and perhaps something can be learnt from reading reviews. I might find out what people like or dislike about my books. Handy to know, I guess. I have read them all; that is, the handful of reviews I have had so far.

Many authors believe Goodreads is only for readers and consequently don't read their reviews there. I don't think I agree. It might be another platform where I can connect with readers. I have followed people who have reviewed my book, and if I get a five-star review, I thank them in the comments. I am uncertain this strategy is useful yet, as I have only just begun to implement it.

I have heard horror stories of how authors have been devastated by particularly nasty reviews. Fortunately, I haven't had a nasty one yet. But I had my first two-star review recently, and it wasn't much fun to read. However, some things that were said gave me something to think about. I know I will eventually read a mean review. But if I can remember that I can't control what others think of my work, and that my books are not for everyone, I think I will be able to deal with it.

And in the meantime, I will just concentrate on the kind reviews and focus on the pleasure and sense of pride I feel when I hold my published books in my hands.

Key Takeaways:

- As a self-published author marketing is an absolute must and relies solely on the author.

- A website and an email list are critical to success. They're the only things that the author can completely control.

- Content marketing such as samples of your work, newsletters and blog posts can be helpful.

- Social media can help but is only a small part of the puzzle.

- Reviews are important but not easy to get.

- There are many options for paid advertising.

Author Talks

Despite my introverted tendencies, I found that I enjoyed doing author talks. The people who attend are really interested in my work and have their own interesting stories to tell. These events are a great opportunity to meet people who might read my books. I have been able to sell quite a few books directly to the readers who attended my talks. Doing author talks has the added benefit of getting books into the libraries that I attend. Goulburn Valley Libraries, Goldfields Libraries and Riverina Libraries all asked me to supply copies so they had them available to lend before I did the talks so, at the very least, I will have books in those libraries. The more people who have access to my books, the happier I am. Not everyone can afford to buy books, and so I am glad that they can borrow them from a library.

Conflict at Hanging Rock

I was excited when I got my first invitation to speak to my family history group about *Conflict at Hanging Rock* soon after it was published. The group meets regularly online on Zoom to discuss a range of topics, and there is also a writing group. This first talk went well, and there were about 15 people in attendance, and the recording was distributed to several more. I felt somewhat nervous, but I was reasonably comfortable in this setting amongst some of the members who I had been meeting online with for some time. It proved to be a great way to start my speaking engagements giving me confidence for other author talks.

The decision to approach libraries was difficult. I composed an email to send to the local Yarrawonga library, asking if they were willing to host an author talk or book signing. It sat in my draft email folder for days, and the actual act of sending it felt horrendous. It took some time for them to get back to me, but fortunately, they were keen to host an author talk.

The local librarians put me in touch with the Program Coordinator who was very helpful and enthusiastic. I was grateful to her because she put me at ease and made me feel like I was worthy of her time and effort in promoting this event for me. She went to great lengths to promote my talks. I guess I shouldn't have been surprised as these are the events that libraries run all the time. But imposter syndrome was rearing its head again, and as a debut author who no-one has heard of, I just wasn't sure I would be acceptable for their program.

I enjoyed that event, after my initial nerves settled, and it was quite successful with about 20 people in attendance – pretty good for my first in-person event.

This gave me the confidence to approach other libraries. I sent emails to libraries around Hanging Rock, where my book is set. I was invited to do talks at the Romsey and Woodend libraries. Once again, these were quite successful and well attended. I also tried to get my books into the gift shop at the Hanging Rock cafe on commission, but that was unsuccessful.

Breaking Free

When *Breaking Free* was published, I once again did a talk at my local library. It was good to see some of the same faces who had attended my first event.

I was also fortunate to connect with the Program Coordinator from the Riverina Regional Library, and she arranged a tour of five libraries in southern New South Wales. It was a great road trip up to places I hadn't been to before, so a lot of fun. I spoke at the Bland Library in West Wyalong, and at the Cootamundra Library. Then, closer to home, I visited the Mulwala, Corowa and Howlong Libraries. Incidentally, that month was my best month in terms of book sales up to that point. The publicity was fantastic for this book tour, with several newspapers publishing articles. They also arranged an interview for me on ABC radio.

Family & Fortune

With my latest novel, I decided to make the launch more of an in-person event, rather than just doing a build-up on social media and a bigger splash on the day of the launch. Once I set the publication date, I contacted the program co-ordinator for our local library and arranged to have the official launch at the Yarrawonga Library. She was better able to promote the event given that it was to be held on publication day. I also decided it was time to get a bit more professional and to put a bit more investment into marketing, so I purchased a banner stand displaying all three books. My cover designer did a wonderful job of the design, and it was a simple matter to get it printed through Officeworks. I felt very proud to set up my stunning new banner stand at all my events as I went around promoting my books.

The launch was a fun event. By now I had an author network, so there were three other authors from our author community in attendance as well as quite a good crowd of locals. Some of these people had attended all three of my Yarrawonga events.

Following up from the launch, I did some more talks in the Riverina Libraries at Tumut, Junee, Coolamon, Leeton and Berrigan. Then, closer to home, I did talks at Tatura and Nagambie.

I certainly found meeting readers and selling direct through library visits enjoyable and worthwhile.

Key Takeaways:

- Author talks are a great way to connect with readers.

- Libraries will often put your books on their shelves if you offer to do author talks.

- Direct selling at author talks can be quite beneficial.

- Creating connections with Librarians and program coordinators makes the task of obtaining author talks easier.

Competitions and Recognition

Competitions are often considered to be a valuable way to gain recognition for your work. As a self-published author, I do not get the validation that comes from having a publisher read my manuscripts. Competitions are another way to get professional eyes on my work. However, I suppose that would only be the case if I were to have some success. I have entered numerous competitions since I began publishing but have not had any success so far.

In 2022, I entered *Conflict at Hanging Rock* in the Dorothy Hewitt Award for an unpublished manuscript.

The next big one I entered was the Historical Novel Society of Australia's ARA Historical Novel Prize. Although the past winners have all been more literary type books as opposed to my more commercial offerings, I decided to enter. The requirements specified historical fiction books published within the past 12 months. I had published books, so why not enter them?

You never know. I entered *Breaking Free* in 2024 and *Family & Fortune* in 2025.

Whilst I was writing *Breaking Free*, I came across the First Pages competition which, as the title implies, requests the first few pages of a manuscript. As I had *Breaking Free* well under way, I thought I might as well give this one a try.

I submitted the cover of *Breaking Free* to the Kobo Book Cover awards in 2023. This was another benefit of publishing my book directly with Kobo as I would not have been eligible to enter this competition if I had published to Kobo through an aggregator such as Draft2Digital.

I have also entered quite a few short-story competitions. I started entering the Australian Writers Centre Furious Fiction competition. But that did not really suit me as there was a 55-hour time limit and specific guidelines and prompts. I need more time to think about the story. However, I entered a few times, when something occurred to me that met the criteria.

Other short story competitions I have entered are the Albury City Council Short Story Competition, Right Left Write run by the Queensland Writer's Centre and, most recently, I entered one in the Write Around the Murray short story competition. I also entered the E. M. Fletcher Award run by Family History ACT in 2023 and 2024. Although I was unsuccessful in winning any prizes in that competition, my stories have been published alongside the other entries in the short story collection they publish each year. Being included in a publication such as this has the advantage that my stories are being read.

I also submitted an entry for the Now Novel Coaching Prize. As you can see, it is not for want of trying. I sometimes wonder whether it is worth the time and effort that goes into competition entries. But for a self-published author, it would be a great way to gain some validation for my work if I could at least make a long list one day. I will keep trying as the opportunity and time arise.

Key Takeaways:

- It is worth entering competitions even if unsuccessful because you never know who might read your work.

- If you don't succeed at first, keep trying.

Part 6: The Business of Becoming an Author

Boughyards Press

Running the Business

When I embarked on the path to self-publishing, I understood I would need to cover all the costs. During my research into the self-publishing process, I quickly came to realise that whilst I wanted to keep control of all aspects of my book, I certainly would not be able to do it all myself. There are ways to lower the costs of publishing a book and some self-published authors do need to minimise costs. They might only pay for minimal editing or purchase a ready-made cover. Some even design their own covers. But they are more skilled than I.

Given that there still seems to be the perception that some self-published books are inferior, I am determined to ensure that I don't contribute to this perception by publishing a less than professional book. I know I will always need help from professionals, at the very least for cover design and editing. These are services I will always continue to pay for, in order to ensure that my books are of a high quality. I started looking into the cost and found that it was going to be substantial. Editing can cost anywhere from $70 to $140AUD per hour. Full print book cover designs can cost between $350 and $950AUD. Knowing all this made me consider how many of my books I would need to sell just to break even. I decided to prepare myself to accept that it was likely that I would lose money in the initial stages.

I needed a coherent plan, so I started work on a business plan and budget. It was originally quite sparse as there were many things I didn't know enough about. However, after many iterations this is how it looks now.

My business plan includes the following headings:

1. Business Summary - This section provides a concise overview of what I aim to achieve from my business. I have set my major goals, which include whether I am aiming for financial success or just the success of becoming a published author. I am fortunate that I don't need my books to make money so my main goal was to get my work published and to gather a group of readers who care about my stories. However a secondary goal is to build up my business by continuing to write more books so that in time it can sustain itself without my continued financial investment.

2. Production - This section lists the products I have available for sale, my publishing schedule and my pricing strategy. Setting appropriate prices is important. I spent some time researching what others were charg-

ing before setting my prices.

3. Marketing - I have attempted to plan my marketing strategy carefully, which was challenging due to the numerous options available. The critical components are the spaces I own, including my website and my email list. Other factors to consider include social media, paid advertising and networking.

4. Professional Development - I determined that one of my top strengths was learning, which I found out by doing the online Clifton Strengths talent assessment. Learning has always proved beneficial in my professional life, but it proved to be even more useful as I became a published author because there are always new things to learn. A plan for continued learning is essential to my success. At present this includes learning to narrate an audiobook and run a Kickstarter campaign.

5. Financial - This section includes my budget and projections. Another consideration was having a business bank account so that I could separate my business and personal finances. I initially put off this important step, but now I have it in place, which will make it easier to keep accurate records.

6. And finally, next steps - I need to review my Business Plan regularly so I set dates to revisit and update it at least every three months.

When I initially completed all this planning, I realised there were quite a few more expenses than I had anticipated.

My author website was the first big expense and was quite substantial even though I did all the work myself. Whilst Squarespace does not offer a free version, it does provide a relatively inexpensive subscription for a basic website. But, as I wanted to sell my books direct from the site, I found I needed to upgrade to the Business version. The fee for my website is over $300 and is charged annually, so will be an ongoing expense. I was also paying extra for email campaigns on Squarespace.

Apart from the website fee itself, there is a fee for domain hosting. I have registered several domain names to protect myself in case someone else tries to use a version of my domain name. It is not an enormous expense, and I think it is worth having the other domains. But it is another expense.

I purchased Scrivener as my main writing application. It has lots of functionality but has quite a steep learning curve. On the other hand, Atticus, which I use for formatting, is quite simple. These products were both available for a one-time fee, which includes upgrades at no extra cost. This is, of course, preferable to annual subscription fees that apply to many software programs.

ISBNs had to be purchased through Thorpe Bowker Identifier Services in Australia. I soon found that it is more cost-effective to buy these in batches of ten.

I paid a small fee to upload my first book to IngramSpark. But I later learned that I did not need to pay that fee. Memberships of writers' associations often offer promo codes for IngramSpark. I am a member of The Alliance of Independent authors and so could have used the code from that. However, IngramSpark no longer charges this fee.

The cost of the courses I have undertaken has also been significant. The Self-Publishing 101 course was expensive at around $800, but as I could pay by installments over 24 months, I decided to enrol. However, I consider these costs, along with the other courses I have completed, to be an important investment that will serve me well throughout my writing career. As previously stated I have also purchased several writing craft books.

I hope to recoup some of these costs one day, but at the time of writing they continue to mount.

Key Takeaways:

- There are many expenses that may not be apparent at the beginning of the journey to become a self-published author. A significant budget is required before embarking on this pathway.

- Business planning is key to ensuring all bases are covered and there are no nasty surprises.

- Business plans are living documents and should be reviewed regularly.

Estate Planning

Where do I start with this one? Nobody knows what tomorrow will bring. It is not a subject that everyone is keen to discuss. But careful preparation and planning can make the process much less stressful. If the worst were to happen, I do not want to leave an untidy mess for my heirs to clean up.

My books are not yet making a profit. At the moment, I would suggest to my heirs that they simply cancel all subscriptions, and wind up the business. But what if the business becomes profitable before I die? I continue to write books and plan to keep doing so indefinitely. At some point, although it feels unreal now, it might be worthwhile to keep the business going, continue the website subscription, do some advertising and maintain bank accounts for any royalties that might trickle in.

This will require careful planning, and recently my family and I discussed what they would want to do after I am gone. One of my children has power of attorney, and she has indicated that she might be interested in continuing the business. However, I do not want to leave a mess for her to clean up.

At least we have started having the conversation. The first steps will be to set up an additional signatory to my business account.

Now that we, as a family, have decided on the best way forward I have adjusted my will to include the succession of my business.

The technology we are all so reliant on in our everyday lives adds another level of complexity. What about all the passwords? I have an online password manager, so only the master password is required to access all my accounts – except for those where the passwords have been changed while not logged in to the password manager. And then there is the issue presented by two-factor authentication, which often utilises biometrics such as fingerprint and face recognition.

The more one considers these issues, the more complex they seem.

The plan is to set up a filing system and spreadsheets, that lists everything someone taking over my business would need to know.

I have a spreadsheet that lists all my subscriptions, including the costs and expiration dates.

Whilst I have made a start, there is a huge amount of work still to do. For the moment, I will let my family know what I have already put in place and what else I plan to do to ensure a smooth succession.

Key Takeaways:

- Estate planning is not a popular topic but taking some

simple steps can ease the stress of the transition.

- It is a good idea to have a clause in your will to clarify what will happen with your writing business.

- Technology and how it is accessed is an important consideration in this process.

Tools of the Trade

I have always loved trying out shiny new technology tools. I know that this can slow down my process, but it is so much fun finding and trying something that will help me complete a task more effectively. Of course, not everything goes smoothly, and there are many times when I get extremely frustrated because I can't get my head around a new technology. However, I generally find it rewarding to figure out a new tool or a process that helps me achieve my goals.

It was certainly not all smooth sailing as I tried to navigate the self-publishing process. I found it fairly challenging, even for someone who enjoys technology. There was just so much to learn. And often the only way to learn is to just give it a go. Whilst I was using tools that only affected me and the manuscript, I was fine. But when it came to working out how to use retailers' sites and populate platforms like Goodreads, I found the process incredibly daunting. I was continually questioning myself. What if I got it wrong? Could I fix it? What if I uploaded my books to Amazon and discovered errors that weren't caught during the editing process or the book cover wasn't the correct dimensions?

All the experts were saying not to worry; you can always just upload another version of your book if you find a mistake. But it just seemed a bridge too far. This led to being ridiculously pedantic about everything. Changing, reverting, never completely satisfied. In the early stages, I wasn't sure I would ever be content with just putting my books out into the world.

I know this all sounds rather off-putting, and I wouldn't want to discourage anyone from giving self-publishing a go, because despite all of my misgivings and fears my books have now been published on a wide variety of platforms. I know that would have been unlikely had I gone down the traditional path.

Now, having come this far in my self-publishing adventure, I can mention some of the tools I ultimately used and highlight some I found particularly useful, along with my reasons for using them.

I use Scrivener to write my manuscripts. It is an excellent program that I discovered quite early in my writing career. Once I got serious, that is. My early work for 'Grandma's Rose' was all simply written in word. I wrote my blog posts directly into the blogging platform I use, which is WordPress. Or alternatively I would write them in Word and then copy and paste them into WordPress. When I discovered Scrivener, I was quite impressed. It was a one-off purchase, rather than a subscription model, and it was reasonably priced. Better still, since I first purchased it, there have been a couple of upgrades, which were free. Like many software programs, Scrivener has a vast array of functionality that I have not yet learned to use and possibly never will. I just use the functions that make the process more streamlined for me. I think everyone has their own preferences about how to use this program. However, the thing I find particularly useful is the ability to move chapters or scenes around by simply dragging and dropping. I can also label scenes with different colours or different icons. There is a section for research. I upload research documents, web links and images so that everything is in the one place. Learning the program was daunting at first because it is quite complex. However, I would highly recommend it. It backs up automatically every time I shut it down. But I also use the compile feature every time I write. This feature exports the manuscript to a Word document. I end up with many Word documents, which I can refer back to if necessary. The backups and word documents are all saved to the cloud in my Microsoft OneDrive.

When I first started writing, I had bits of historical knowledge gleaned from my research floating around in my head. But when I needed to refer back to the source, it took ages to find what I needed, resulting in a lot of wasted time. Lately, I have tried to keep track of where I have found everything. Some of this is saved in the Scrivener research folder.

I also like to use OneNote in the Microsoft Suite for taking notes and conducting research as I can access it easily on my phone or any of my devices. My OneNote has numerous notebooks and notes covering all aspects of my research and the writing process, including inspirational quotes and excerpts, ideas for blogging, stories, newsletters and a myriad of other topics. I appreciate the simplicity of being able to access these resources in one place from all my devices.

I have also done some writing in another program called Atticus. I purchased this software, which was also a one-off subscription for the formatting process. In fact, I mainly use it for the formatting. There are lots of templates that format the book however you like. There is also the capacity to change the templates. Once I have finished the formatting, I can download the book as an ePub for the ebook, PDF for print and also a simple Word document. I always download as a final copy in Word so I have a workable document that I can use for any last-minute changes. I find Atticus to be a nice, simple writing tool. It was quite basic when I first purchased it, but they are adding new features all the time. Basic is sometimes a good thing because the learning curve is not quite as steep. I listened to a podcast where the creator of this tool discussed the additional features they would be adding in the future. Their long-term aim is to provide a program that can be used from start to finish of the book writing and publishing process. A writing, formatting and editing program all rolled into one. It sounds like it will be amazing if the developers manage to complete everything they are hoping to. It should be a one-stop shop for all areas of writing a book. Lately, they have implemented the ability for collaboration. Beta readers and editors will be able to add markup within the program. When I first heard about this function, I was quite excited because early information indicated that collaborators would not need an Atticus account. However, when I asked my beta reader to trial this function, she found that not only did she have to have an account but there was also a subscription cost involved. This is disappointing as I don't see how it will be useful unless beta readers and editors happen to use Atticus for their own writing or editing. I am hoping that the developers eventually allow beta readers and editors to have access to my manuscripts without having to pay.

ProWritingAid is the program I use to check grammar, style and spelling. It is not a free tool, but when I first purchased it, there was a reasonable annual subscription fee. Later, having found it to be extremely useful, I purchased a lifetime license. It is a powerful program, and I always use it before I send my work to my editor. I have also used Grammarly, but I think ProWritingAid probably has more features. A new version has recently been released, which uses AI to provide a beta reader report and a full developmental report. I haven't had a chance to try it yet. But even if I do find it useful for self-editing, I will always continue to use a human editor for the main editing process.

I can use ProWritingAid in conjunction with Scrivener, which I found really useful. This is only available with the paid version. After downloading the desktop app, I was then able to open my Scrivener project directly in ProWritingAid. All the changes are saved in Scrivener.

My website is on the Squarespace platform. It is an adequate platform, but not without its drawbacks. It is quite expensive to begin with. I have also heard that Wix is good platform and cheaper. I may try that in the future. But for now I am reasonably happy with Squarespace. It has also recently included an upgrade, which allows much more flexibility with easy-to-use drag-and-drop features. One of the really annoying parts is the blog. I find it inflexible when it comes to adding images to a post. I think the blog post function in Squarespace needs to have a bit more creativity and flexibility to enable photos, diagrams and content other than just plain text to be added more easily.

As previously mentioned, I first used MailChimp for my newsletters. It is a great email platform, but once you need more features than they offer in the free version, it is quite expensive. For one thing, even though I had a paid website subscription, I wasn't able to link it to Mailchimp, so I had to set up a Google Doc to receive subscriptions from the website and manually add them to my subscriber list. This, of course, was not ideal. I switched to MailerLite. It is a straightforward platform. I particularly liked the automation function on MailerLite because of its simplicity. Unfortunately, it does not integrate with Squarespace, so I still had to manually collect and enter email addresses from my website. I decided to try out Squarespace for email so that email subscribers would automatically be added to my list. However, it does not have the functionality of the programs that are specifically designed for email newsletters. And there was an additional annual cost. My most recent experiment is to try Kit, yet another email marketing platform, which I am still learning to use. It is free for the first 10,000 subscribers and I am sure it will take me a long time to reach that number. My first newsletter in 2026 was sent with Kit. I am not entirely sure why I have not been able to settle on one platform. I hope this is the one.

Another piece of software I invested in was Publisher Rocket. When uploading to the retail sites, you need to add categories and keywords. Publisher Rocket saves a lot of time when determining what the best keywords are for uploading a book to Amazon. It also helps to find books that use a particular keyword and determine how to compete with them. Finding the correct categories on Amazon can be tricky, as when uploading a book, only a tiny selection of the available categories are shown. I needed to drill down to the least competitive categories. It is quite a complex process, but apparently helps to improve discoverability on Amazon.

BookFunnel is a simply magnificent all-round platform for distributing ebooks. Without it, I could not sell my ebooks direct from my website. It is a simple platform to learn, and all you need to do is upload your ebook and cover and then create a landing page. The link can be sent to the reader. They also help readers who may struggle to work out how to download the book. The basic plan is excellent value at only $20 USD per year. That plan has so far provided everything I need. However, if I want to distribute audiobooks via BookFunnel I will need to go to a higher plan. There are other benefits of BookFunnel.

Users can create group promos and organise author swaps at no additional cost. Plus, they now offer a Universal Book Link (UBL) that can link not only to retail stores but also to my website. I can use that link to direct customers to my books on all retail sites, so that the reader can purchase from their preferred store. Of course, I always hope that they will purchase directly from my website.

Draft2Digital is the aggregator I use to distribute my ebooks to the retail stores. They do not charge a fee to distribute the books, but rather they take a percentage of the sale price when a book is sold.

I discovered a great little tool called Google Ngrams. One of the conundrums of writing history is whether a word or phrase that we might use today was in common use in the relevant time period. This tool allows you to enter a word or phrase, and it gives an indication of whether the word or phrase would have been in everyday use at a specific time in the past.

Canva is one of my most used tools. It is a fantastic design tool that I use extensively for creating marketing assets. There are many templates that can be used. I have a paid annual subscription because it is especially useful. I also used Canva for the video editing of my book trailer.

There are so many useful tools, many of them designed by writers for writers. Some have a steeper learning curve than others, but I have found all those mentioned here useful.

Key Takeaways:

- When struggling with new software it can be helpful to

leave it for a time and return later, as sometimes there is a glitch on the program or another solution might occur.

- Whilst some are more user friendly than others, all the programs and platforms take time and patience to learn.

- Look for programs and platforms that are created by writers for writers. There are plenty of them available.

Part 7: Looking Ahead

Boughyards Press

Other Projects – Creating a Family History Book

A project that was very close to my heart was the family history book I published as a gift for my mother's 90th birthday. This is why I started writing in the first place – to tell my family stories. It was a truly joyful project.

As my mother's 90th birthday approached in March 2023, I considered trying to complete my factual account of my family history, which I had begun writing many years ago. It is currently titled 'Grandma's Rose', a nod to a rose we all have in our gardens and my grandmother's gardening skills. However, when I realised I would never finish it in time for this momentous occasion, I decided to leave it on the back burner and focus on a project that I knew I could complete to a high standard in the available time.

I wrote and published the story of her early life, as well as that of her direct ancestors, parents, siblings and descendants, including her children, grandchildren and great-grandchildren. This project was such a delight to work on, complete with images and family trees. At least that part of the family history is faithfully recorded. But there is so much more of the story still to tell.

It was a totally different type of work from my novels. I wanted it to be well-designed, with full colour, and include lots of pictures. Thankfully, I came across a course that taught me everything I needed to know about putting the book together. A Canva book template was included in the course.

I had to set some boundaries for this book because there are so many stories and so many ancestors I could write about. I started with my mother's immediate family, her siblings and parents. Then I added her descendants: four children, 10 grand-children and 7 great-grandchildren – the last of whom was born in January 2023, just in time to be included in the book. Then, for her ancestors, I chose to include only her direct line, going back only as far as the first immigrants to Australia.

Once I had it designed to my liking, I then had to work out how to publish it. I didn't intend to sell it outside of the family. This being the case, I didn't need to consider how to distribute it. It was simply a matter of determining the best way to get it into print. The options I had used for my novels would not be suitable for this book, because it includes many images.

My first attempt was with Lulu, a print on demand self-pub-lishing platform that does photo books, calendars and a range of other products. This looked like a good option. Unfortunately,

I didn't realise it had to be printed in Jamaica, so it took over a month to arrive. But more importantly, the quality was not great. In fact, some pages came loose almost immediately. I have since heard good things about Lulu, but unfortunately that was not my experience.

My next choice was Blurb, similar to Lulu, producing photo books. This presented another problem as the available sizing did not match the format of my book. I had to go back to Canva and resize the book. But in the end, the finished product was excellent and was delivered promptly. After we presented Mum with her copy, other family members also wanted a copy. This was a simple process. As Blurb is print on demand, I could order the exact number of copies I needed. Since that time, other members of the extended family have also ordered copies.

As is often the case with these works, no matter how closely you edit and proofread, there will always be mistakes. As the family read the book, these came to light. I have produced quite a few editions, but I think it is now as accurate as it can be given my knowledge of the family history as it stands now. There is always more to discover, of course. For those with the earlier editions, I have typed up a list of the errors, copies of which I have inserted into each of the books.

My mother and my extended family were all delighted with the book, so it was an incredibly rewarding project. I now need to do one for the paternal side of the family. It will be another enormous project that I will need to schedule soon.

Key Takeaways:

- Factual family history books are quite different to a fiction novel, so require a different process.

- A good template is useful.

Artificial Intelligence

The use of Artificial Intelligence (AI) by authors is a controversial subject. I will say upfront that I do use AI. But I use it to support, not replace, my writing skills and ideas. The characters, the story and the finished manuscript remain my own work.

The recent growth of AI has had a tremendous impact on every facet of our lives. The rate of growth since ChatGPT was launched in late 2022 has been astronomical. For authors and other creatives, it has meant that their work has been scraped from the internet and used to train these Large Language Models. This, of course, is not fair. Creatives have copyright over their work and should be compensated if it is used by a third party. As previously mentioned, my social media site of choice has been Instagram. It has come to light that Meta, which owns both Instagram and Facebook, has admitted to using the database of a pirated book website to train its AI model. This caused considerable angst among authors.

Unfortunately, as is often the case with technological advances, regulation has not kept up with the rise of AI. There are many court cases proceeding that will help to determine fair use, but all this takes time. Licensing deals are being explored, and several big organisations have struck up deals with AI developers such as OpenAI, which created ChatGPT. There is a lot to roll out. However, one thing is certain, AI is not going away.

I use AI in my work and have done so ever since I started writing, way back in 2019. I use ProWritingAid to check my spelling and grammar. Many other software programs incorporate elements of AI. And the number is ever increasing, so I do not see any way I can realistically escape using AI in the future. Even if I wanted to, which I now must admit – I don't.

There are significant benefits in using ChatGPT, Claude, Midjourney, Perplexity, Ideogram, Runway and many others. I have used AI to create marketing images. It has helped me to write marketing copy and to craft book descriptions. I have also used it to help me come up with new ideas.

I think it is perfectly acceptable to feel conflicted about AI; that is, to have concerns about its direction, whether it will replace all our jobs, and any number of other concerns. Already, AI can write reasonably well if prompted efficiently. But on the other hand, I feel excited by the significant benefits that AI offers. Some believe that AI will steal our creativity, but personally, I find it helps me to think more critically and enhances my creativity. I find that I need to use my creativity and clear thinking to design efficient prompts and to get the best from these models.

I created a book trailer for my most recent book, *Family & Fortune*. Now, before I explain how I did that with the help of AI, I need to stress that I simply would not have been able to afford to have a book trailer if I had not been able to use AI. I feel it is for this purpose that AI becomes more important. For things that would not have been created otherwise.

I had a lot of fun creating the book trailer. I followed the process that Joanna Penn described for her Patreon subscribers, relying heavily on AI.

First, I asked Claude AI for a plan for my video. Then I asked for some prompts that I could use in Midjourney (an image creation AI platform). I created all the images and then up-loaded them to Runway, where I could transform the still im-ages into video. Finally, I uploaded these small videos to Canva and stitched them all together with transitions and added text to each screen. Incidentally, I had to do quite a bit of editing to the text provided by Claude and I also had to re-generate the images in Midjourney multiple times before I got what I thought was appropriate. I certainly had to use my own creativity.

Audiobooks are another notable example of the benefits of AI. To get an audiobook published using a well-known human narrator costs thousands of dollars. For me, that is just out of the question. Without AI, having my books published in audio format is not a real possibility. I do hope that in the future, as my business becomes more profitable, I will be able to afford to have a human-narrated audiobook. But for now, that is a pipe dream. I used auto narration in Google Play to create audiobooks. The standard was not great when I first did that back in 2022. However, the technology for audiobooks, like all artificial intelligence, is improving at a rapid rate. Currently, I am deciding whether to take auto narration further. There is a relatively new audio platform called ElevenLabs, which from all reports is excellent. I intend to give that a try.

For now, I remain conflicted about AI, but I will definitely stay informed as the almost daily changes and updates occur, so that I am not left behind with this mind-blowing technology.

Key Takeaways:

- AI is here to stay. It cannot be put back in the box so, at the very least, I believe we need to become informed.

- It is perfectly okay to be conflicted about AI as there are pros and cons.

- Whether or not you use AI in any of your writing or business processes is up to you, but it can be extremely useful.

Where to From Here

I consider myself a writer first and foremost, not a publisher. So, the best way to make a career as a writer is to write more books. I need to keep writing and publishing and continue to build my body of work. I cannot afford to rest on my laurels.

But having said that, of course I am a publisher as well. I need to take that role seriously and treat my writing and publishing as a business. I have found that many hours need to be spent on the business side, which eats into my writing time. I am yet to find the balance between these two necessary but competing pursuits of a self-published author.

If I could speak to my 2019 self, when I commenced writing *Conflict at Hanging Rock,* I would tell her this:

You do not need to know everything before you begin. You will learn by doing and making mistakes. You will worry more than you should, about whether you are doing it correctly. But mostly the worry will turn out to be unnecessary. You will feel exposed when you share your work but that vulnerability is where connection begins. And most importantly, I would tell her that starting imperfectly is not a flaw, it is the only way anything worthwhile gets written.

So, where to from here? There are still many stories I have discovered in my family history research that I want to write about. My next project will be the story of the Boughyards family, who immigrated to Australia from Ireland in the 1860s. I have always wondered why they waited so long after the Great Famine of 1947 to come to Australia. Hundreds of thousands of people immigrated in the so-called coffin ships travelling to North America and Australia during the potato famine. Yet my family stayed in Ireland for approximately 15 years after the worst of the famine was over. My story will explore that question along with the trials and tribulations the family endured on the voyage out and continued to endure when they did finally arrive in Australia.

I also plan to write the story of my grandmother and her brother George, which will be a sequel to both *Breaking Free* and *The Boughyards*. This is where two branches of my family merge. But I am finding this too close to home at the moment. I knew and loved my grandmother very much, so I am struggling to think of her in a fictional sense. Everyone else I have written about so far came from earlier generations, long dead, and whom I never knew. But I hope to eventually honour her by telling her story.

Then there are those projects that I have begun but still not finished. The stories that will be just for family. I want to finish

'Grandma's Rose' and also the family history book for my father's side. I have plenty of material for each of these projects, so I need to make time to get them completed.

Another exciting adventure awaits me in 2026. My sister and I will be travelling to Ireland, Scotland and England. This is a big thing for me as my overseas travels have never taken me further than Thailand. We will be visiting many of the places of origin of our family. Recently I discovered the church where Mary Ann and Richard, who feature in *Family & Fortune*, were married still stands in Luton. I can only imagine the surreal feelings that a visit to this church will evoke. It will also be amazing to visit County Kerry in Ireland where my father's side of the family originated. I am sure it will bring some of his stories to life. I have already mentioned the benefits of visiting the places where my novels are set, so this will be such a special experience, which I am very much looking forward to. I am sure the trip will add richness to my upcoming stories.

As my writing improves, I would like to expand my horizons. Once I become a little more established as an author, I plan to branch out to write in other genres. I love cosy crime, having read and enjoyed many Agatha Christie mysteries. So, this is one genre I would like to explore. That would be a whole new learning curve, of course. I think perhaps I might write a historical mystery.

But having said all that, I am branching out here with this non-fiction memoir. This manuscript is my first long non-fiction project. I believe I could be quite proficient at writing non-fiction given that a significant portion of my writing during my earlier career has been in this area.

My goal is to launch this book via a Kickstarter campaign. I have just finished reading **How to Launch Your Book on Kickstarter** by Russell Nohelty which, whilst providing a wealth of information, has really made me question this decision. It appears that it will take an immense amount of time and effort to launch this way. But I would really like to give it a go.

As the years go by, I wonder how much of this I will be able to accomplish. There is still so much to write and to learn. I plan to live a long, healthy life, but who knows what the future holds? For the moment, I will ignore my advancing age and continue to write.

Becoming an indie author did not simply give me books with my name on the cover. It changed my perception of myself. I no longer wait for permission to begin. I know that learning something new does not have to be uncomfortable. More and more, I understand that mistakes are not signs of failure but rather opportunities to learn. Writing has strengthened my resilience and my patience and given me a quiet confidence that I can finish what I start.

If this book does nothing but encourage one person to begin, whatever doubts they may hold, then it has done its job.

Now that you've finished reading Becoming an Indie Author, it'd mean the world to me if you left an honest review on your favourite platform. Even leaving a star rating makes a world of difference.

Acknowledgements

Once again I need to thank many people who have contributed to this book. But this is a little different to my other books because, whilst there are several people who have assisted me in the usual ways, many others have helped without even necessarily being aware of the fact.

Firstly, and as always, I must thank my editor, Cecile Shanahan. Cecile has been my editor from the beginning and has lifted every one my books to a standard that I could never have achieved on my own. I am deeply grateful, once again, for your dedication and guidance.

Beta readers are the best! They are the ones that can tell me whether the story comes together in an engaging way. Once again I would like to thank Hannah McCarthy who has read all of my manuscripts and always provided useful and insightful feedback. This occasion is no different. Thank you also to Sandra Wiles, Chrissie Bellbrae and Susan Mackie for their generous and perceptive comments

Douglas Thomson from High Voltage Studio did a superb job of the cover as usual. Thanks again, Douglas.

As you read you will see that I have mentioned many authors from whom I have learnt so much and who have supported me along the way. My thanks go out to all of them.

I would particularly like to mention the Write Squad Community and the Writes4Women group, both of which I have leant on for support and encouragement as this book came together.

And finally, I want to thank you, the reader. Without readers, we authors would be nothing. I am extremely grateful for each and every one of you.

Resources

The following software and tools are those that I have used and which have worked well for me:

- Scrivener – the program I use for writing. Lots of functionality but some learning required.

- Atticus – book formatting software for both ebook and print. Simple to use for basic formatting but has additional functionality available.

- BookFunnel – distribution of ebook and audio books. Especially useful for direct sales or giveaways.

- Kit – Email program.

- Rocket Publisher – assists with finding appropriate categories and keywords for Amazon.

- Squarespace – website.

- Canva – Excellent design tool with lots of templates.

- Kobo – ebook and audiobook retailer.

- Kindle Direct Publishing (KDP) – retailer for Amazon for both ebook and print.

- Draft2Digital – Aggregator which distributes widely to many ebook retailers.

- Ingram Spark – Aggregaor which distributes widely to many retailers.

- Ngrams – a tool to determine usage of words in a particular time period.

- Blurb – for publishing books that have lots of photos.

Books that have inspired me:
- Kin by Nick Brodie

- Searching for Charlotte by Kate Forsyth and Belinda Murrell

- Hard Times by Charles Dickens

- The Mayor of Casterbridge and Far from the Madding Crowd by Thomas Hardy

- Save the Cat Writes a Novel by Jessica Brody

- So You Want to Be a Writer by A L Tait and Valerie Khoo

- The Writing Book by Kate Grenville

- Blueprint for a Book by Jennie Nash

- The Novel Project by Graeme Simpsion

- On Writing by Stephen King

- Reading Like a Writer by Francine Prose

- Look it's Your Book by Anna Featherstone

- Author 2.0 Blueprint and Successful Self-Publishing by Joanna Penn

- How to Launch Your Book With Kickstarter by Russell Nohelty

9 781763 828216